EFFECTIVE COMMUNICATION

Educated at St Paul's School, John Adair has enjoyed a varied and colourful career. He served in the Arab Legion, worked as a deckhand on an Arctic trawler and had a spell as an orderly in a hospital operating theatre. After Cambridge he became Senior Lecturer in Military History and Leadership Training Adviser at the Royal Military Academy, Sandhurst, before becoming Director of Studies at St. George's House in Windsor Castle and then Associate Director of The Industrial Society.

In 1979 John became the world's first university Professor of Leadership Studies at the University of Surrey. He holds the degrees of Master of Arts from Cambridge University, Master of Letters from Oxford University and Doctor of Philosophy from London University, and he also is a Fellow of the Royal Historical Society.

In 2006 the People's Republic of China conferred on John the title of Honorary Professor of Leadership Studies in recognition of his 'outstanding research and contribution in the field of Leadership'. In 2009 the United Nations appointed him to be Chair of Strategic Leadership Studies at its central college in Turin.

www.johnadair.co.uk
www.adairleadershipdevelopment.com

EFFECTIVE COMMUNICATION

THE MOST IMPORTANT
MANAGEMENT SKILL OF ALL

JOHN ADAIR

PAN BOOKS

First published 1997 by Pan Books

This edition published 2009 by Pan Books
an imprint of Pan Macmillan Ltd
Pan Macmillan, 20 New Wharf Road, London N1 9RR
Basingstoke and Oxford
Associated companies throughout the world
www.panmacmillan.com

ISBN 978-0-330-50426-3

1 3 5 7 9 8 6 4 2

A CIP catalogue record for this book is available from
the British Library.

Typeset by SetSystems Ltd, Saffron Walden, Essex
Printed and bound in the UK by
CPI Mackays, Chatham ME5 8TD

CONTENTS

INTRODUCTION

Communication skills are essential in leading, managing and working with others. The aim of this book is to help you to improve your competencies and capability in the art of practical communication.

An understanding of the NATURE OF COMMUNI-CATION is the foundation, and this is the subject of the first chapter. This is followed by THE COMMUNICATION STAR, a useful model of framework. The historical case study in Chapter 3 gives you an opportunity to apply what you have learnt so far.

The four skills of SPEAKING, LISTENING,WRITING and READING form the themes of Chapters 4, 5, 6 and 7. Of course we all have grounding and ability in these skills, and so it is more a matter of sharpening and honing them in the context of daily working life. If you aspire to lead or manage others you do have to be really competent in these skills, because communication is the brother and sister of leader-ship. The Five Principles of Good Speaking, which also double up as general Principles of Communication – BE SIMPLE, BE PREPARED, BE CLEAR, BE VIVID and BE NATURAL are also introduced in these chapters. It will serve you well to tie these principles firmly to your mast as they can be applied to all forms of communication and hence come up throughout the book.

Four situations that pose problems of communication in

which you will find yourself as a leader are discussed in Part Three. PRESENTATIONS are formal speeches; they usually involve audio-visual aids and are sometimes done by more than one speaker working as a team. INTERVIEWS are essentially one-to-one meetings with a purpose. From the communicating angle, perhaps the most difficult aspect is giving and receiving praise and criticism. Managing communication in group MEETINGS is obviously an essential part of any manager's work. Lastly, ORGANIZATION – the general situation or context of managerial work – solves some communication problems but creates others.

It follows that to be an effective communicator, you need to develop an understanding of your PERSONAL skills, your ability to lead communication in GROUPS and your effectiveness in the downward, upward and sideways flows of information and ideas in ORGANIZATIONS – including, of course the interactions of the organization with its customers. Here, then, are the contents at a glance:

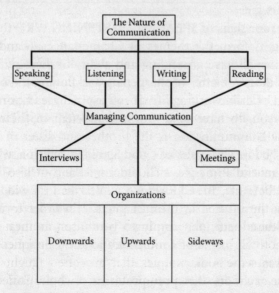

Remember that the purpose of the following pages is to stimulate your own thoughts and ideas about communication at work. They should lead you to identify some practical ways in which you can improve your skills both as a communicator and as a manager of communication.

HOW TO USE THIS BOOK

In order to benefit most from this book it is best to read it once to get a general understanding of its contents. Then go back and work through the checklist questions and exercises. If you can persuade a friend or colleague to monitor your answers, even better.

Do not assume that you have to start from the beginning and read through to the end. Even within a chapter you may prefer to complete the checklist before reading the chapter, rather than afterwards. Decide your strategy for using the book now, according to your depth of interest and preferred method of learning.

I suggest that you have a pencil and paper at hand when you study the book more closely. Write down any action points. And don't be afraid to write on the book – I won't mind! Underline or mark any passages that are important to you personally in terms of your own AWARENESS, UNDERSTANDING and SKILL.

This book will give you guidance not only on when to communicate and why it should be done, but also how it should be done. It is concerned with skills in a wide sense, namely the methods you must practise in order to achieve your desired aim of becoming a better communicator. But this book will not teach you much about techniques in the narrower sense – techniques that are often taught at the expense of the art of communication as a whole. Concentrate on the basics – and leave the tricks-of-the-trade to the charlatans.

In order not to hold you up unnecessarily on your first fast-track read, you'll find some material – relevant research and other contributions – in boxes within the text. Again, be selective about them. You can skip past a box without any loss to the main themes of the book if you prefer.

The key points at the end of each chapter are designed to give you an aide-memoire of the whole contents. Just to keep you on your toes I have occasionally slipped in one or two extra points – ones you won't find in the preceding chapter.

I hope you enjoy reading the book as well as finding it useful and profitable. I have certainly enjoyed writing it.

John Adair, 2009

PART ONE

UNDERSTANDING COMMUNICATION

1

THE NATURE OF
COMMUNICATION

'The peoples of the world are islands shouting at
each other across a sea of misunderstanding.'
George Eliot, English author

These words remind us that lack of communication is
endemic in our human condition. Loud shouting and even
violence are symptoms of the ailment, not remedies. Without
communication we remain isolated, stranded on our islands,
divided rather than united. To diagnose the nature of communication is as important for us now – as individuals,
groups and nations – as the discovery of the secrets of the
atom was for our grandfathers. We have to discern the forces
that create human unity – not those that split matter with a
crash – invisible forces that can conquer the 'sea of misunderstanding' and bind our hearts together. The technical
problems of long-range communication have been solved;
the more central and elusive nature of good communication
in human relations remains to be charted.

But what does this long, formidable word 'communication'
mean? Some verbal archaeology may help. Using the *Shorter
Oxford English Dictionary* in this case, we can unravel the

meanings that the word 'communication' has acquired down the centuries. First, it comes from the same Latin root as 'common', namely the word *communis*, whose own roots are shrouded in mystery. The first part of it presents no difficulties, for 'com' is known to be an English version of *cum* (with). The second part, *munis*, descends either from *moinis* (bound), or from the early Latin *oinos* (one). Dr Samuel Johnson, author of the *Dictionary of the English Language* published in 1755, defined the first and major family of meanings of the word 'common' thus: 'belonging equally to more than one'.

Our medieval forefathers used 'common' as a verb much as we use 'communicate' nowadays. Until the beginning of Queen Elizabeth I's reign in the mid-sixteenth century, an Englishman might have spoken of 'commoning' with his friends about his work, rather than of 'communicating' with them. However, 'commoning' might equally have meant that he was eating with friends at a common table in the great hall of some manor house or college, pasturing his pigs on the common land, or partaking in the Holy Communion or Mass at the parish church. Behind all these uses is the central idea of *sharing*: something is available for all to share in it. Thus it is general and not private, a joint rather than an individual possession, one which is accessible freely to others.

'To communicate', a verb that entered the language about the time that Henry VIII was having problems with his six wives, took over the dual senses of giving to another as a partaker and making available something for a general sharing. 'Communication' came to mean the action of imparting, conveying or exchanging or, more concretely, that which is communicated, such as a letter or its contents. Although the Christian religion has retained 'communicate' and 'Communion' for the sharing of the sacramental elements of the Eucharist, the words are now rarely used in regard to material things. Almost exclusively, communication now refers to the giving, receiving or sharing of ideas, knowledge, feelings – the contents of the mind, heart and spirit of man – by such means as speech, writing or signs.

Quite early in its history, however, communication took on the extra job of denoting the access or means of access between two or more persons or places. By 1684 the word was used to describe an alley or passage; much earlier, in the English Civil War, the trenches and ramparts connecting the star-shaped forts around London were called the 'lines of communication'. When an army campaigned in the field its lines of communication were the routes or means that linked it with base and with other allied armies: the roads, rivers or canals that made possible the essential communication or sharing of intentions, information and results. The term 'communications' now covers all the latter-day additions to the primitive trench or passageway: telegraph, telephone, radio, television and computer. The distinguishing feature of all these modern inventions is that they enable rapid communication between persons widely separated thus giving them the group name 'telecommunications', with 'tele' stemming from the Greek word for 'far off'.

So we may fruitfully distinguish three strands in the pedigree of communication, each of which still colours our use of the word. First, it means that which is shared, the 'commons', be they bread, land, ideas or life itself. More specifically, as the English language flowered, communication stood for the action of sharing in the mental or non-material realm, especially in and through the use of words. Lastly, anything that links two or more persons or places has come to be called a communication. In other words, communication has come to include the means used as well as the primary activity itself.

Communicating usually implies both intention and means. In a sharper focus we could say that communication is essentially the ability of one person to make contact with another and to make himself or herself understood. Or, if you prefer a slightly more formal version, communication is the process by which meanings are exchanged between people through the use of a common set of symbols.

Intention and a common set of symbols – usually combined to form a language – are immensely important factors but they should not be allowed to fill the whole picture. Emotions or feelings, for example, are non-material. They are certainly communicated, sometimes intentionally but more often not. Nor is a common set of symbols involved. Emotions often do not need words. You should always bear in mind this much broader backcloth of communication, which encompasses such phenomena as the unintentional and direct transfer of states of mind or feelings.

You can see that there are four elements implicit within it. Of course, the whole process will always be more than the sum of these four parts but each of them is an important factor in the overall story. In the table below, I briefly identify them and this is followed by an outline of their characteristics.

KEY INGREDIENTS IN COMMUNICATION	
KEY ELEMENT	**NOTES**
Social contact	The persons who are communicating have to be in touch with each other
Common medium	Both parties to communication must share a common language or means of communication
Transmission	The message has to be imparted clearly
Understanding	The message has to be received, properly understood and interpreted

THE ROOTS OF COMMUNICATION

We can perhaps learn more about the distinctive nature of communication in humans if we glance first at the world of animals, birds and fish. Wherever we look in the animal kingdom we find that communication through the senses is less liable to error than in man, but it is much more limited. Humans, with our infinitely richer potential, are capable of attaining a communion with our fellows and universe, which is beyond the reach of even the most developed animal. Yet our communications are much more likely to go awry than those of our evolutionary cousins and our more distant relatives in the family of the living.

In her pioneering study of chimpanzees, *In the Shadow of Man* (1971), the zoologist Jane van Lawick-Goodall emphasized that speech sets humans far ahead of their nearest primate cousins but that we retain many of the primitive methods of communication observable in the chimp. Some of her thoughts are as follows:

In fact, if we survey the whole range of the postural and gestural communication signals of chimpanzees and humans, we find striking similarities in many instances. It would appear then, that either man and chimp have evolved gestures and postures along a most remarkable parallel, or that we share with the chimpanzees, an ancestor in the dim and very distant past; an ancestor, moreover, who communicated with his kind by means of kissing and embracing, touching and patting and holding hands.

One of the major differences between man and his closest living relative is, of course, that the chimpanzee has not developed the power of speech. Even the most intensive efforts to teach young chimps to talk have met with virtually no success. Verbal language does indeed represent a truly gigantic stride forward in man's evolution.

All the same, when humans come to an exchange of emotional feelings, most people fall back on the old chimpanzee-type of gestural communication – the cheering pat, the embrace of exuberance, the clasp of hands. And when on these occasions, we use words too, we often use them in rather the same way as a chimpanzee utters his calls – on an emotional level.

It is only through a real understanding of the ways in which chimpanzees and men show similarities in behaviour that we can reflect, with meaning, on the ways in which men and chimpanzees 'differ'. And only then can we really begin to appreciate, in a biological and spiritual manner, the full extent of man's uniqueness.

A chimpanzee or an otter, however, are less likely to misinterpret one of their kind touching or clasping them in the presence of some anxiety-producing threat than, say, a young woman whose hand is suddenly held by her neighbour in a descending aeroplane. The repertoire of signs, gestures and postures is limited and all the animals seem to know the code.

The nature of humans greatly confuses the issue. Not only is our speech an infinitely varied weaving and interweaving of forty different sounds but the resulting words are capable of many different interpretations. Hence a man or woman can convey or communicate much more widely and more deeply than a chimp can with his fellows but at the risk of being more misunderstood and more isolated than any in the animal kingdom.

The limitations of animals can be further illustrated by considering the following conditions that are necessary if they are to learn even the most elementary lessons:

- The response expected must not be unduly complex; the animal must be able to reach the food or escape the danger by making reasonably simple movements. In other words the problem must not be too difficult.
- The lesson must be presented to the animal under conditions that ensure freedom from extraneous disturbance. An animal will not learn if its attention is constantly diverted by other changes in the environment.
- The problem must be presented on an adequate number of occasions; the more frequent the lesson the fewer the mistakes.
- There must be an 'incentive' to learn – a reward for success or a punishment for failure. Further, the reward must be related to the needs of the animal.
- Finally, the experimenter must possess adequate skill and patience. Ability to learn depends to a very large extent on the personality and enthusiasm of the teacher.

Humans far transcend animals but we can trace some of the roots of human communication in such experiments: namely that the factors of content, situation, method, subject and teacher must all come into play. Certainly simplicity and repetition retain their value in all instruction or learning. But there is another legacy from our evolutionary past. Despite our development of language we retain non-verbal communication as an important auxiliary system.

NON-VERBAL COMMUNICATION

The basic system for communication is the human body; not only the organs of speech and hearing but eyes and facial muscles, hands and arms, brain and in many respects the entire body. Caressing, embracing and holding hands are as much ways of communicating as human speech. Body language, as it is now familiarly called, is something we both use and observe throughout our waking hours. Everyone, for example, can interpret a smile or a threatening gesture. And the voice conveys more through its tone or volume than simply the words spoken.

We can distinguish at least nine ingredients in this 'undercover language' of non-verbal communication. They are:

- Facial expression
- Eye contact
- Tone of voice
- Physical touch
- Appearance (clothes, hair)
- Body/posture
- Proximity
- Physical gestures – hand and foot movements
- Head position

Take eye contact, for example. Video film of conversations shows that the talker tends to look away while actually speaking but glances up at the end of sentences for some reaction from the listener. This usually takes the form of a nod or murmur of assent. He or she gives the listener a longer gaze when the talk has finished.

For the most part this undercover language is a natural or unconscious expression of our feelings, synchronized with what we are saying or doing consciously.

It follows that one can only change non-verbal behaviour by changing the inner nature that it is expressing. Courses or conferences that aim to teach you what Shakespeare called 'the craft of smiles' are to be regarded with suspicion, although help can be given to those whose synchronization has become dysfunctional.

Courses for normal people in such matters as eye contact or gesture could only induce self-consciousness, which works against natural communication. What is important, however, is the *awareness* that other people are receiving all our non-verbal behaviour, and perhaps finding it expressive of certain unseen inner states or attitudes that may or may not be there. One can legitimately strive to avoid sending out the wrong signs or signals through the variety of non-verbal channels.

Fortunately, we now have language, which can in part rectify our mistakes. But it is the original integrated combination of words and signs that makes up the rich texture of human communication. We must now turn to our unique capacity for communicating through language – the prime means of human intercourse.

COMMUNICATION AS DIALOGUE

Most people seem to regard spoken communication as getting a message across to another person: you tell him or her what you want him or her to know. This concept implies a one-way traffic from one person to another, with all the emphasis being on transferring a message from one mind to another. Of course we all do this constantly, for example when we tell a taxi driver our destination. But there are some people who have a semi-conscious theory that this is what communication is all about. If this theory is combined with an ingrained self-centredness, it can produce the phenomenon of 'the bore': one who insists on monopolizing the conversation to transmit *their* messages, regardless of the needs or interests of their hearers. Bores are an ancient social scourge. In 1611 the dictionarist Randle Cotgrave could define a 'monologue' as 'one that loves to hear himself talk.'

In its strict sense 'monologue' means speaking alone. It became a theatrical term for a scene in which a person of the drama speaks alone and hence to its modern use of a dramatic composition for a single performer. By the mid-nineteenth century it had extended its meaning to cover all talk or discourse that resembled a soliloquy. In theoretical terms, the word 'monologue' implies today an emphasis upon one-way communication, with a corresponding lack of awareness of the importance of dialogue, namely of listening as well as speaking, of sharing instead of giving.

'Dialogue', which means literally a conversation between two or more persons, comes from the same Greek verb as 'dialectic' – the art of critical examination into the truth of an opinion. In early English, dialectic was simply a synonym for 'logic' as applied to formal rhetorical reasoning; in later philosophy it began to take on shades of meaning that still colour its use in our time. The German philosopher Georg Hegel (1770–1831) applied the word dialectic to the process of thought by which the mutually contradictory principles of science, when employed on objects beyond the limits of sensory experience – for example, the soul, the world or God – are seen to merge themselves in a higher truth that comprehends them. Thus we may speak of a dialectic as a method of critically inquiring into truth, one in which a dialogue between apparently conflicting views is more appropriate than a reflective soliloquy by a lone thinker.

It is important to distinguish between monologue and dialogue as *methods* of communication on the one hand, and as *theories* or *assumptions* about communication on the other. There is room for a diversity of methods but we need to constantly rediscover the essential unity of the nature of communication as a shared or common activity. If you close your eyes now and stop reading you will effectively end the communication between us. You are involved in it as much as I am: we are partners in crime. Somehow I have to lead you to make up the deficiencies in my book with your thoughts. If one of us fails, then the communication falls to the ground. The real fallacy of the monologist philosophy is that it ignores your and my contribution to the communication process. Monologue sees us as a passive audience; dialogue knows that the other person holds some of the cards that will give to or withhold meaning from both of us. Truly communicative people want to know as much about the person or people with whom they wish to communicate as they do about the subject in question.

Consequently an awareness of the other person or persons as active contributors to the 'commoning', and not as passive receivers, is an unseen dimension that can influence any form of communication. Sometimes it is difficult for the learned or wise to believe that their listeners or readers have anything to add except 'Amen'.

'The monological argument against the dialogical process is that the ignorant and untutored have nothing to contribute, so that the addition of zero and zero equals zero,' wrote pastoral studies professor Dr Reuel L. Howe in *Herein is Love* (1961).

This kind of comment, which is made by surprisingly intelligent and otherwise perceptive people and too often by educators, demonstrates how little they know about the processes of learning. Nor does it follow that the dialogical principle forbids the use of the monological method. There is a place for the lecture and for direct presentation of content, but to be most useful they should be in a dialogical context. Furthermore, it is quite possible for a person giving a lecture to give it in such a way that he draws his hearers into active response to his thought, and although they remain verbally silent, the effect is that of dialogue.

As a matter of fact, one should not confuse the different methods of teaching with the dialogical concept of communication. Both the lecturer and the discussion leader can be either monological or dialogical even though they are using different methods. People who believe that communication, and therefore education, is dialogical in nature will use every tool in the accomplishment of their purpose. When the question needs to be raised, they may use the discussion method or perhaps some visual aid. When an answer is indicated, they may give a lecture or use some transmissive resource. But their orientation to a task is based on the belief that their accomplishments as leaders are dependent partly upon what their pupils bring to learning, and that for education to take place the relationship between teacher and pupil must be mutual.

Dialogue is nothing more than good conversation: two persons face-to-face, talking and listening to each other, perhaps using gestures and signs as well. Seven characteristics of such conversations have been suggested. They are:

- Face-to-face
- A two-way process
- Informal
- Sincere and open
- Adapted to the situation in which it occurs
- Constitutes a means to an end
- Desired and enjoyable

Communication tends to be effective in situations that resemble the direct face-to-face conversation and less effective the less similar they are. If one person cannot see the other something is already lost from the equation. Dialogue stands close to the heart of communication.

FEEDBACK

A major contribution to our understanding of communication has come from the introduction of the concept of *feedback*. Norbert Wiener, the US applied mathematician and founder of cybernetics, coined this term in 1946 in an influential book entitled *Cybernetics: or Control and Communication in the Animal and the Machine*. In it he compared communication to a system that loops back on itself: the parts are linked together in a cycle of activity like a child's electrical train set. Information does not just pass downwards or outwards: it curves backwards like a boomerang and affects the communicator. This phenomenon of bouncing back, the return of information through the system, Wiener called *feedback*.

This model, an instrumental metaphor from the electrical and electronics fields, emphasized the *two-way* or *dialogue* character of communication. According to this picture, communication was a process in which the sender received *feedback* from the hearer that might lead him or her to

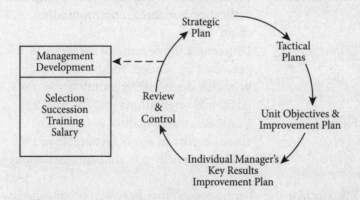

The role of feedback

modify their approach. In diagrammatical terms the nearest representation to the model was a circle, and various forms of the circular model such as ovals and rectangles with rounded corners became popular in the early management literature. There are many versions of it, but the essential idea is the same. The example above of the feedback process comes from management expert John Humble's book *Improving Management Performance* (1969).

It has been hoped that the circular model as shown above would portray communication as flexible, dynamic and democratic, as indeed to some extent it does. Moreover the electronics background to this systems model provided some good metaphors for failings of communication in personal and organizational life. They include:

Timing	Coordinating messages in such a way that they are received either simultaneously or sequentially by different receivers
Overload	Reception of messages in such quantity that the receiver is overwhelmed and unable to respond intelligently
Short-Circuiting	The omission of one or more persons in a vertical or horizontal communication chain
Distortion	Differences in meaning of messages as perceived by senders and by receivers, primarily due to different job or positional orientations
Filtering	Conscious manipulation of 'facts' to colour events in a way favourable to the sender (especially upward communication)

The circular or systemic model does have certain drawbacks. Circles and systems can imply a concentration on social maintenance. The cyclic model also evokes some prevalent and largely unexamined assumptions about the nature of society and meaning of history. The circular image of things returning to their starting points like the change of the seasons has never entirely satisfied Western civilization. For better or worse we want to push onwards along a line into the unknown. 'Better fifty years of Europe than a cycle of Cathay,' the English poet Tennyson declared in the nineteenth century.

KEY POINTS: THE NATURE OF COMMUNICATION

- The concept of communication embraces a wide range of meanings that circle around the idea of *sharing*. That sharing or exchange is now more commonly related to abstract things, notably meaning.
- For communication to happen there are some necessary elements or conditions: social contact, a common medium, transmission and understanding.
- Some contact or connection is required. It may be physically close or, through technology, at a distance. If you are out of touch with people you can't communicate with them. But you may be out of touch because you don't communicate! Communication creates relationships; relationships produce communication.
- Although we have evolved language as our principal medium for communicating with each other, we retain non-verbal communication – just as a sailing yacht might have an auxiliary motor. It is especially important as an expression of relationship. In Japan as in African tribal society, for example, how near or far you sit from the door indicates your seniority.

- Both a distinct and clear transmission of some kind is required, and also an equal reception of it. Both 'sender' and 'receiver' contribute to the process by which meanings are exchanged between them by a common system of symbols.

> *Communication is the art of being understood.*
> Peter Ustinov, British actor and dramatist

2

THE COMMUNICATION STAR

'We cannot live only for ourselves. A thousand fibres
connect us with our fellow men; and among those
fibres, as sympathetic threads, our actions come as
causes, and they come back to us as effects.'
Herman Melville, US author

In the first chapter of this book the importance of the
receiver as a positive contributor to the achievement of
understanding is emphasized. But there are other elements
involved in the 'commoning' of any matter. In this chapter
these elements will be identified and discussed with the help
of the model I call the COMMUNICATION STAR.

The point of this model is that it visually illustrates the
essential inter-relatedness of the elements or aspects of communication. But it is far from perfect and you may be
prompted to build your own model by its very inadequacies.
In other words, its purpose is to keep you thinking, not to
bring our discussion to a halt.

There seem to be six key aspects to communication. First,
there is the *communicator* – the person who has something to
share. Secondly, there is the intention or *aim* that lies behind
the communication. Thirdly, there is the other person or

persons, the receivers or *communicants*. The *content* or matter of the communication – whatever it may be – forms the fourth main ingredient. Fifthly, the means or *methods* of the communication constitute an independent element in their own right. Lastly, the context or *situation* in which it all takes place influences the nature and outcome of all communication.

These six aspects or elements stand in a complex relationship of interaction with each other, as we shall see when we look at the salient factors to be considered under each heading.

We tend to regard them from the viewpoint of the communicator. One way of developing understanding of communication is to look at it from other viewpoints. We could imagine the elements as billiard balls that can be sized up from different angles. Or possibly as the outer points and centre of a star, joined and defined by lines of relationship as shown in the figure below:

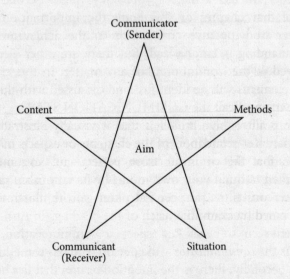

The Communication Star

It is tempting to put arrows on the linking lines in the diagram above and to make it into a dynamic process. But this would be oversimplification, a return to the one-way traffic idea. The influences between the points are tidal: they ebb and flow in both directions. Thus the diagram is alive in that it moves, contracts and propels itself forward in time and space like an amoeba but unlike that amorphous creature there are the six 'elements' to which the mind can constantly return: *aim, communicator, communicant, content, methods* and *situation*.

What then are the relationships between these variables? Obviously there is some sort of relationship between sender and receiver – *communicator* and *communicant* – but quite what character it has will vary: in fact it will always be unique. There is also, or ought to be, a relationship between the *content* and *methods* but again the nature of the link between them will vary very widely from instance to instance. In fact a major proposition might be that all six factors have a complex interconnection with each other and that in studying any one instance of communication we are looking at a particular pattern of relationships between them. You could picture this as a skein of wild geese flying in line then changing formation into a new pattern arrowed across the evening sky.

Thus all of them are connected with each other, albeit by a somewhat roundabout route in some cases. We may postulate that the communication is likely to be good when there are strong and positive lines of relationship defining all six constants. This general point can be illustrated and confirmed by examining each of the headings in turn.

THE AIM

Ideally the *aim* should stand at the centre of the star, shared by the persons concerned and served by the content, methods and situation. If the intention is only in one person's mind and remains obstinately there without moving out into the middle then the work of communication is unlikely to be successful. The art of communication lies largely in creating a sense of a common aim. Communication is not two people gazing into each other's eyes; it is two or more looking together at a common question, problem or opportunity. In other words it is a means to an end.

The word 'aim' is to be understood here as standing between *purpose* and *objectives* on a scale ranging from the abstract to the concrete. A purpose is a general direction, a broad river fed by – and feeding – its tributary aims and small stream objectives. The latter are usually concrete *goals* or *targets* that are designed to be achieved in some tangible way and in a short space of time. An aim need not be quite so concrete or short-lived: it unites the sweep of the large purpose with the earthiness of objectives and hence can well stand for the intentional heart of human communication.

Usually it is possible to define one's aim in terms of the results that should follow from the communication. These may fall into broad areas, such as change, commitment, action or understanding. It is then necessary, if possible, to break them down to more specific objectives by asking '*What* change?', 'Commitment to *what*?' or 'Understanding *what* in particular?'

Besides working *downwards* from the key words denoting aim or intention, it is also necessary occasionally to work *upwards*. The ultimate purpose of all human communication may be threefold: to further the common enterprise of humanity; to create and express unity; and to build up the personal lives of individuals. The overlap between these three areas, ever changing as the centrifugal and centripetal forces press it with tensions, may be what we recognize as true peace – the legitimate end of all good communication.

THE COMMUNICATOR (SENDER)

The efficacy of any communication will depend in part on the quality of the communicator or sender just as music varies with its performer. Thus he or she is one element in any analysis of communication. We are not only the musicians, we are also the musical instruments. The quality and tone of our instrument is made up partly from such more-or-less fixed attributes as our personality, character, intelligence, experience, age and sex. These attributes, which go into the making of an individual person, are not inanimate pieces of matter: they are living and pulsating, always transmitting their own signals and always colouring our intentional messages with the distinctive sound of the whole person.

Here we come up against the first major factor in the communicator. Perhaps the majority of our communications, as in the cradle, are involuntary: they are the radio waves transmitted ceaselessly by the heartbeats of our conscious and unconscious or depth minds. We do not need Sigmund Freud to remind us that we communicate much more than we imagine we do. Perhaps because communication is so essential for survival and evolutionary progress, nature has given us an overplus of communicatory powers. Just as our breathing is involuntary so is our communication with one another. Indeed if we stopped communicating altogether we should die.

Some textbooks write as if communication resembled

archery: you carefully select an arrow, flex your muscles, feel the wind, eye the target and then shoot. But communication is not entirely like shooting arrows; it resembles more a bubbling, singing, sometimes roaring, mountain stream, which flows endlessly and is never silent whether we will or no. The task of the communicator is to harness this surging outward-flowing river within him, so that it turns dynamos and lights up the city or adds to the natural reservoirs of common knowledge. This we can do because we are human and personal, not animals or things.

The differences in our make-up are the result of our genetic inheritance and upbringing on the one hand, and how we have responded to them on the other hand. We could say that each of us has a certain inherited potential as a communicator, which a good education will spotlight and develop. This is especially true where the essentials are concerned: the ability to think and to express thought simply, clearly and vividly in words or pictures.

If we carefully studied a highly effective natural communicator – and perhaps we have all met such a person – we should observe that first he or she is able to share fully what is in their mind if they wish to do so. As far as the involuntary – or natural – communication is concerned, what comes across either accurately supports what he or she is consciously saying or else expresses his or her personality and character in a not unpleasing harmony, although it may strictly be irrelevant to the present matter. The involuntary communication does not conflict with what is seen or heard: there is no jarring dissonance.

Thus the natural communicator is highly adept at using the dams and turbines of language as well as non-verbal pictures and signs to convey his or her meaning. But, as the image of the dam suggests, they are also capable of holding something back.

Paradoxically, natural communicators are also masters of the art of *not* communicating. Much water may find its way around the dam but it is filtered and sometimes checked in the light of the communicator's general stance or attitude to life and their particular aim. Like a skilled artist he or she knows instinctively what lines to leave out of the picture.

Our education and training in realizing our potential as communicators begins as soon as we are born. We are conceived and born into a communication system – the family – that we both complicate and enrich. The fundamental skills, at least to a rudimentary level, we acquire early and retain all through our lives. Thus a potential for communication that is always greater than we ever use, and some form of education and training for developing the complex and all-embracing faculty are our birthrights. We evolve the ability because we need it, but the possession of the ability also strengthens the need, like a perpetual-motion machine. This brings us to another major factor in the communicator: the *need* to communicate.

The natural need to communicate varies greatly in strength from individual to individual, but it is present in some degree in all of us. It furnishes the shadowy background to the more specific and conscious motives or intentions that lie behind actual communications. Our motive for these, the everyday communications at work or home, are a mixture of a subjective and general need to communicate with the more objective necessities of the situation. Where those objective necessities, emanating from outside ourselves, are weak or non-existent, then we either communicate for the sake of communicating or we remain silent. The natural communicator may naturally prefer the second, less popular, alternative.

Thus much of what passes for communication is really the verbal or visual expression of the need for communication.

Nothing is being said but we are conveying the message that we can talk, that we are human. The need is a natural one, and we become anxious if we meet someone who consistently betrays no need to communicate at all. But we also have to protect ourselves against those with such a strong need to communicate that they impose themselves upon us. We have to guard ourselves against becoming a 'sounding brass or tinkling cymbal'.

Therefore in our profile of 'humans as communicators' we may distinguish between three elements. First, there is the *inherited potential*. It includes both the species-wide faculties such as the seeds of thinking and speaking, and the individual's birth inheritance. This inheritance includes particular aptitudes for handling different kinds of ideas and the extent and range of verbal facility. Nobody can make a silk purse out of a sow's ear.

Secondly, the *influences* of family, society and culture, coupled with the quality of the skill-training of early school days, combine to shape us into persons with a certain level of ability for communication. Doubtless Stradivarius chose the best wood for his violins but so did other violin makers. Yet something went into the making of a 'Stradivarius' that transformed all the potential of wood, gut and varnish into a masterpiece for conveying the violin music of his day. We are all different instruments, each specialized for a purpose, but we should all be capable of playing a simple tune. Beyond that it takes the ear of a master to judge special qualities.

Thirdly, to switch over to the woodwind and brass sections of the orchestra, there is the wind in our lungs and our need to blow it out. We are all communicators in that we need to communicate as we need to expire the breath in our chest. The musician can contain that breath for longer than most of us; he or she is trained to direct it correctly and can also refrain from always playing the trumpet. He or she has become a musician first and foremost and only secondly a trumpet player or flautist.

So we are capable of being communicators and not just talkers or scribblers. But the cost of becoming so is precisely our ability to discipline our tireless need to communicate; to harness it to truly human and personal ends or let it flow sometimes into the reservoirs and cisterns of silence. We have to manage our need to communicate or be managed by it: there is no compromise.

THE COMMUNICANT (RECEIVER)

We all have an inborn potential to recognize meaning in the messages that come to us. We are natural communicants. But we do not all receive the same messages in the same way. Our receiving apparatus is like a computer in that we bring a store of patterns and ready-made interpretations to the work of listening, watching or reading. This transforms the receiving of communications from a passive to an active and positive occupation. As the US author and naturalist Henry David Thoreau said: 'It takes two to speak truth – one to speak and one to hear.'

The sense of meaning is the raw material that makes us into communicants. This capacity to find or give meaning we take with us wherever we go. For some external stimulus to become a communication we have to pick it up on the constantly scanning radar screen of our consciousness; then it has to blaze a light of meaning on that dark hidden inner screen. It is our capacity to perceive meaning that makes us into *Homo sapiens*.

Culture and education shape our sense of meaning into certain ranges of 'meanings' and 'interpretations' that we carry with us in more-or-less ready-made packages. At a low level there are simply classifications: the idea of a 'tree' is in my mind and it leaps to consciousness if I am asked to name the image of that tall swaying thing just outside my window as I write. At a higher level we are capable of filling in, from our own stocks of accumulated meanings, the various signs, signals and symbols that convey messages or meanings to us on frames of reference as fragile as snowflakes.

'Perception' comes from a Latin word meaning 'to lay hold of thoroughly'. Prior to the late seventeenth century, like communication, it could also describe a partaking in the Eucharist. Eventually, however, it came to be used for taking in, or receiving through the mind or senses, again rather like a communication itself. We also use it today to describe the ability to apprehend or grasp what is not present to observation, to see through or to see into the less obvious nature or significance of something or someone. The latter may include an intuitive recognition of value, be it moral, aesthetic or utilitarian.

Thus perception, the faculty of perceiving in all these senses, gives us a good idea of the range of contribution that the communicant may offer. He or she may simply take and receive what is given, through the faculty of comprehension. They may interpret something that is not immediately apparent. Or they may have to penetrate inside an opaque communication with a laser beam of intellect. This is always necessary when the communicator does not know what he or she is trying to say. They may think they do, but even the offering they have measured and cut may contain flaws and grains beyond their own range of understanding, just as a drug may have side effects unbeknown to the administering doctor.

Moreover, to the alert receiver the stream of involuntary and largely non-verbal communication may suggest much about the hidden contents of the communicator's mind, the broad base of the iceberg whose surface shape is being presented for inspection and purchase. Of course it is precisely in these higher reaches of perception, where the rewards are greater, that the communicant is more likely to misunderstand, mistake and misread the message so tantalizingly veiled from him or her.

THE CONTENT

Much writing on communication stresses the importance of the skills of the communicator and the receptivity of the communicants. Granted these essentials, so it is believed, the message cannot fail to pass from one to the other. The latter – the receivers – hold the aces because they are the ones who hallmark the communication with a stamp of meaning. Meaning is subjective; it is given or bestowed by the recipients.

But it may not be quite as simple as that. We certainly all do possess the faculty of *valuing*, the magnetic force that is inwardly attracted to value and meaning. Yet it only contributes half the sum. We need something that has value in it, as an intrinsic property. Although philosophers will continue to debate whether values can be objective in that sense, and the prevailing fashion is to regard all values as the result of projections of meaning from the individual or the social mind, the subjective theory does not work when it comes to the practical business of communication. In the marketplace of ideas we do tend to judge whether the products up for auction are true or not.

This is a vital point because it removes the whole subject of communication from the realm of what the English philosopher Francis Bacon called 'cunning' and what we should describe as techniques or even gimmicks. It has been

my observation that truth does somehow have its own power
to communicate. It is as if what is true, or even contains
some grains of truth, is like radioactive dust: it has power to
transmit its own signals, regardless of its bearer. If the
evidences of truth are not present the message may be
accepted for a time but its mortality is assured.

Thus part of the secret of communication is to find
something that is true to say – and then let it speak for itself.
The fact that the content, or rather the truth in the content,
is speaking will make the communicator into a listener and
a receiver of their own message. It is possible to dress up
material in the clothes of truth but the proof lies in the
eating of the pudding. Quite where we came by this particular value lining to our depth minds – what I call the deep
part of our mind where much of our analysing, synthesizing
and valuing goes on to help bring ideas to the forefront – I
do not know. But we do have a natural power of responding
to the power of truth and an armoury of weapons – some
primitive and some highly sophisticated – for penetrating
the surfaces and appearances of the conversational and
communicative 'food' that is presented to us.

The life of a message therefore lies in the truth of its
content. The more true it is, gold that is refined or pure, the
longer it will be retained in the minds of at least some of the
hearers. The communicator is not one who seeks to convey
his or her meaning from their own mind to the minds of
their listeners. He or she is a person who has seen or foreseen
some reality, unearthed some facts, discovered some laws
and theories, which for them have the ring of truth. For a
variety of reasons they wish to share their discovery of this
self-transmitting piece of truth with others. Whether or not
there is agreement will not necessarily determine the truth
of the matter. They may stand against the world and be
proved right. 'The truth is great and shall prevail', wrote the

English poet Coventry Patmore, 'when none care whether it prevail or not.'

Communicated 'meals' come in various categories of digestibility, however, and the communicator may justly 'flavour' the facts. Like children we sometimes have to be tempted to eat. The mind tends to grasp, accept and retain the simple, logical, known and concrete more than the complex, confused, unknown and abstract. It likes an appetizer or aperitif. Short attractive meals, presented at intervals with plenty of time for digestion in the depth mind, are preferable to dull food replete with truth presented at one gargantuan feast. But it is the truth in the food that matters ultimately, not how palatable it happens to be. Only truths are digested by the mind; lies or half-truths always await eventual excretion.

THE METHODS

The fifth element in communication is the *means or methods* employed. Mistress of all intercourse is language, followed closely by pictures. These are all marks or signs upon paper or in the shape of noises that we use to convey a concept from one mind to another, to share our apprehension of reality. Within the family of language there is a variety of 'readymade' constructs to hand, the forms made available by our history: conversations, speeches, essays, books, lectures, presentations and letters.

Technology has lengthened the arms of these readymade constructs in the 'tele-' cluster of inventions, just as printing and the introduction of the Internet has vastly extended the range of the written word.

These methods or forms – the earthenware jars that carry the action of our communications – also have a life of their own. They are like beasts of burden – horse, oxen, mules or camels – that are pressed into service yet retain their own strengths and weaknesses. Sometimes, like fractious animals, they attempt 'to put the cart before the horse' and take over. Once, when riding in the Jordanian desert, I found myself on a semi-wild camel that periodically insisted on bending its swan-like neck to bite me. Methods of communication are like that, always trying to buck you off their backs. The means is always potentially in a state of tension with the end; the form declares war on the content.

Methods or means of communication should not dazzle us by their variety or win us by novelty alone. Like old clothes some of the ancient forms of communication are still the most comfortable, practical and serviceable. We cannot avoid using some method or other and they usually involve language in either the written or spoken versions. But there is an area of choice here. We may not be able to choose what to say, but we can select from several possible ways of saying it.

The general principles governing the choice of means stem from the other elements in the star-shaped pattern of communication, for lines of relation tie them together. First, the communicator should be skilled in that particular medium: it must be part of their repertoire. Skill in one form or medium does not ensure a uniform quality in others. We all develop natural preferences for the elements in which we feel most able to express what is in our mind. Our own history of success and failure in communication predisposes us towards certain methods in which we have developed competence and confidence. But our range is always too limited: there is endless room for self-improvement.

Secondly, the method selected must serve the content; it must be appropriate to the matter in hand. It should not call attention to itself but set forth the content in question in a selfless way. The prime quality of any means of communication is that it should be *fitting*. We can get by with adequate method, but the communicant's mind pays an extra bonus to the communication if the form is perfectly adapted or appropriate to the end. Thus we may properly speak of 'the art of communication' for art largely consists of allowing the content to shine through the medium.

Thirdly, the method must match the receivers or communicants. There are methods appropriate to age groups and occupations, educational levels and attainments. The receiver has certain expectations as to the methods that he or she will employ. Surprises may bring delight, but only if the 'staple diet' is conventional. It is important to know the ways in which the customer likes his meals served to him. The uncommon may be more readily received if it is purveyed in a familiar pattern, be that story, lecture or article.

THE SITUATION

The *situation* in which the communication takes place also exerts its own distinctive influence. Burning decks, for example, are not the best places for long homilies. On the other hand a university campus almost invites lectures. In other words, some methods are more appropriate than others to the actual time and place where the communication occurs.

Of course we can often predict the situation fairly accurately. Providing the communicator has some imagination, he or she can see in their mind's eye the situation, just as they may be able to sum up in advance the characteristics of the receiver or audience. But, although they may grasp the general situation fairly well, the factors in the specific location can change either dramatically or subtly, like the weather. Hence the communicator needs to be flexible: he or she has to be prepared to reset their sails when the wind changes, or even take them down altogether and run before the storm.

The situation of communication has little or no power to render the actual communication satisfactory, but it has considerable potency for throwing spanners in the works. Motor mowers outside the window, the endless clinking of coffee cups, a noisy air conditioner, an overenthusiastic heating system, Arctic cold: the list of distractors is endless. Not only do these attack attention, which is the giving of our minds to the content before us, but they also interrupt the two-way flow of traffic between communicator and communicants. A good communicant may regard such obtrusions as challenges, as occupational hazards to be overcome. But, being human, he or she may be irritated, especially if the distractions or difficulties could, in principle, have been avoided.

The situation, however, can have a positive and benevolent influence, albeit a limited one. Old buildings, for example, may acquire a certain atmosphere, a tone of their own, which blends in with the message. If the communication is about contemporary matters, then a bright new building may reinforce the up-to-date theme.

Would President Lincoln's famous address at Gettysburg have sounded quite the same if it had been delivered in the White House garden? Most of the memorable communications of our history have been given in situations that serve as settings for these rare jewels. To summarize: in effective communication the situation is managed so that all the potentially troublesome factors are eliminated; in the best communication the situation supports and encourages the exchange of minds by its silent witness. The communicator, like a good general, is one who chooses his or her battlefield, and if that cannot be arranged he or she knows how to employ suitable tactics to minimize its shortcomings and maximize its advantages.

SUMMARY

Some aspects of communication we share with other living creatures, especially our ability to express meaning through non-verbal means. Compared with the animal kingdom our means of communication are far greater but the obstacles are greater too. Alas few of us ever experience the heights of personal communication, as in a truly great love for example, but we all catch glimpses of our unrealized possibilities. We can make a start towards the 'promised land' by grasping that communication means *dialogue* and *not monologue*.

Yet when we look more closely, there is more involved than just two personal centres sharing a common interest or intention. In all human communication there seem to be six major factors involved: communicator, communicant, aim, content, methods and situation. All can serve or hinder the aim. All communication is a pattern of lines or relationships between these points:

COMMUNICATOR: A communication in the deliberate or conscious sense implies a person or persons who sends a message.

COMMUNICANT: If in the language of grammar the sender is the 'subject' then the receiver is the 'object' to whom the message is directed.

AIM: The intention of the message is the purpose in the sender's mind for sending it; it is the reason why communication is taking place.

CONTENT: The substance of the message, its component ideas, facts and less obvious value contents.

METHODS: How the message is conveyed, by writing, speaking or using signs, for example.

SITUATION: The context or environment in which the communication is taking place.

If one of the above is totally absent, it stands to reason that there would be no communication. The star-shaped diagram is the result of drawing lines of equal length and spacing or arranging the points in order. That simple exercise demonstrates that, although we have to accept the nature of communication as it is, we can bring order into chaos by grasping the intrinsic factors in each of the six aspects or 'ingredients' and manoeuvring them constantly into the right relation or *proportion* with each other in order to serve the aim. The star suggests order in place of chaos: it represents a vision or ideal where all aspects of communication are completely right, and the issue is a communion of spirit, mind and action. We shall probably never reach this star but we all need it for navigation. The Communication Star may thus serve to remind us to consider always the overall pattern of communication, never just one aspect in isolation from the others.

KEY POINTS: THE COMMUNICATION STAR

• Good communication requires an understanding and skilled *communicator*, presenting a true and necessary *content* to an alert and able *communicant*, using the most appropriate *methods* in a *situation* that is contributing to the meeting of their minds, so that the *aim* is fully achieved.

- You can use the Communication Star as a practical framework when planning for any meeting. If you get it right, there should be a near-perfect harmony between the five elements in relation to the *aim*.
- Examine the true purpose of each communication. Always ask yourself what you really want to accomplish with your message.
- Be mindful, while you communicate, of the overtones as well as the basic content of your message.
- When it comes to content, bear in mind the enduring value of truth in any human communication. As one Ethiopian proverb says: 'Over truth there is light.'
- Consider the total physical and human setting whenever you communicate. Check your sense of *timing* against the situation. *There is a time and place for everything.*
- Take the opportunity, when it arises, to convey something of help or value to the receiver.
- Be sure your actions support your communication. Words should interpret what is done and action should accompany words. Eventually our words should become acts and our acts our truest words.
- Seek not only to be understood but also to understand – be a good listener.

> *Truth has such a face and such a mien,*
> *As to be loved needs only to be seen.*
> John Dryden, *The Hind and the*
> *Panther* (1687)

3

CASE STUDY:
THE FATAL ORDER

'Theirs not to reason why,
Theirs but to do and die:
Into the valley of Death
Rode the six hundred.'
Alfred Tennyson, English poet

The proverbial schoolboy knows the story of the heroic but useless 'Charge of the Light Brigade' at the Battle of Bala-clava: 670 horsemen charged on that fateful afternoon of 25 October 1854; 247 men were killed or wounded and 475 horses slain. The immediate cause of the disaster was the misinterpretation of a written message. But behind that failure, so graphically described in the extract that follows from Cecil Woodham-Smith's book *The Reason Why* (1958) lay a history of strained relations between those who would have to communicate with each other in action.

You may like to space out on a sheet of paper the six elements of the Communication Star and note the factors under each heading that contributed to the tragic destruction of the Light Brigade.

Lord Lucan (Commander of all the cavalry) and Lord Cardigan (the Light Brigade General) had thirty years of quarrels behind them. More recently, Lord Lucan and Captain Nolan (the messenger) exchanged hot words before Balaclava. And these weak personal links must be set against the general lack of 'team maintenance' or cohesion between staff officers and line commanders, infantry and cavalry, and the English and French allies. Thus this glaring instance of bad message writing and passing was but the tip of an iceberg of poor communication; it was upon this cold rock that the Light Brigade foundered.

To appreciate and learn from this disaster it is necessary for the reader to know the essentials of the situation. The Russians in the Crimean War were attempting to intervene in the siege operations before Sebastopol (namely the siege in that city) by cutting the British lines of communication to the seaport of Balaclava. The successful charge of the Heavy Brigade and the stubborn defensive resistance of some infantry regiments checked the Russians. But then Lord Raglan, the Allied Commander, spied the enemy attempting to remove some abandoned guns from some high grounds to his right. The country is hilly and divided by valleys. Raglan's command post was on the high ground at the head of the long winding North Valley. The Russians occupied the heights on either side of it and over a mile away, at its other open end, their cavalry was regrouping behind twelve guns. The Light Brigade stood quite near Raglan but almost on the floor of the valley (see figure overleaf).

Throughout the story it may be helpful for the reader to keep bearing in mind the simple fact that it was the guns on the Causeway Heights that Raglan wished the Light Brigade to secure – not those guarding the Russian cavalry at the end of North Valley. How did Lucan set out towards the wrong objective – and to tragedy? Cecil Woodham-Smith's account

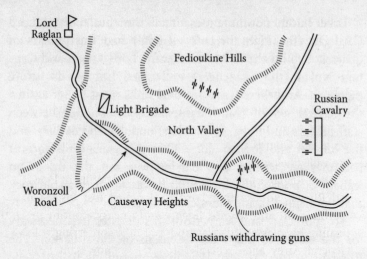

Plan of battle

is worth studying closely; it is an unforgettable parable of bad communication:

The charge of the Heavy Brigade ended the second period of the battle. The aspect of the action had been entirely changed by Scarlett's feat. There was no longer any question of the Russians penetrating to Balaclava, they had been pushed away from Balaclava, even out of the South Valley altogether, and at the moment their position presented difficulties. They held the Causeway Heights and the redoubts, and they had infantry and artillery on the Fedioukine Hills on the other side of the North Valley, but between them the North Valley, 1,000 yards wide, was empty of troops. The troops holding the captured redoubts on the ridge of the Causeway Heights had therefore little support, and Lord Raglan saw that this was the moment to recover the redoubts, the Causeway Heights, and, with the Heights, the Woronzoff Road.

The two divisions of infantry ordered down two hours

earlier should now have come into action, but, though the 1st Division under the Duke of Cambridge was present, the 4th Division under Sir George Cathcart lagged behind. He was still in a bad temper, and as he unwillingly left the Heights, General Airey had brought him orders to assault and recapture the redoubts – So! he thought, his division, straight from the trenches and exhausted, was to attack, while the Guards were merely marched in support along the valley below. He refused to hurry.

Lord Raglan's anger was evident; indeed, William Howard Russell noticed that Lord Raglan had lost his usual marble calm and seemed fidgety and uneasy, continually turning his glasses this way and that and conferring with General Airey and General Estcourt. He now sent Lord Lucan a third order, of which two versions exist. The copy which Lord Raglan retained in his possession runs: 'Cavalry to advance and take advantage of any opportunity to recover the Heights. They will be supported by infantry, which have been ordered to advance on two fronts.' The order as it reached Lord Lucan and was retained by him is slightly different. The final sentence is divided into two. After the word 'ordered' there is a full stop and 'advance' is written with a capital 'A', so that the final words read 'They will be supported by the infantry which have been ordered. Advance on two fronts.' The change does not affect the issue. Lord Raglan expected Lucan to understand from the order that he was to advance and recapture the redoubts at once without waiting for infantry support, but that infantry had been ordered, and could be expected later.

Lord Lucan read the order in precisely the opposite sense. He was to advance when supported by infantry. Not only did the words of Lord Raglan's order seem to him to have this meaning, but Raglan's treatment of the cavalry throughout the campaign made it highly improbable that he would order an attack by cavalry alone. Again and again, at the Bulganek, at and after the Alma, on October 7th, the cavalry had been restrained, recalled, forbidden to take the offensive, prohibited from engaging the enemy. Only an hour or so ago Lord Raglan had withdrawn the cavalry from their position at the entrance to Balaclava, where they were preparing to engage the Russian cavalry, and placed them in an inactive position under the Heights. It never crossed Lucan's mind that he was expected to launch an attack by cavalry with the prospect of being supported at some future time by the infantry. He mounted his division, moved the Light Brigade over to a position across the end of the North Valley, drew up the Heavy Brigade on the slopes of the Woronzoff Road, behind them and on the right, and waited for the infantry, which in his own words 'had not yet arrived'.

Ten minutes, a quarter of an hour, half an hour passed, and the infantry did not appear. Three-quarters of an hour passed, and still Lord Lucan waited. The attack which Lord Raglan wished the cavalry to make appeared to border on recklessness. Redoubt No. 1, on the crown of Canroberts Hill, was inaccessible to horsemen. Nos. 2 and 3 would have to be charged uphill in the face of infantry and artillery. The Heavy Brigade had earlier come within range of the guns in No. 2 and had been forced to retire. However, Lord Raglan, with his power to divine the temper of troops, perceived that the whole Russian Army had been shaken by the triumphant and audacious charge of the Heavy Brigade and that, threatened again by British cavalry, they would retire. Conversations with Russian officers after the war proved Lord Raglan to be right. A feeling of depression had spread through the Russian Army as they saw their great and, as they believed, unconquerable mass of horse-men break and fly before a handful of the Heavy Brigade. For the moment the British possessed a moral ascendancy, but the moment must be swiftly turned to account, and up on the Heights there were murmurs of impatience and indignation as no further action followed the triumph of the Heavy Brigade, and down below Lord Lucan and the cavalry continued to sit motionless in their saddles.

Suddenly along the lines of the Causeway Ridge there was activity. Through glasses teams of artillery horses with lasso tackle could be made out; they were coming up to the redoubts, and a buzz of excitement broke out among the staff. 'By Jove! They're going to take away the guns' – the British naval guns with which the redoubts had been armed.

Captured guns were the proof of victory: Lord Raglan would find it difficult to explain away the Russian claims to have inflicted a defeat on him if the Russians had not only taken an important position, but captured guns as well. The removal of the guns must be prevented, and, calling General Airey, Lord Raglan gave him rapid instructions. General Airey scribbled an order in pencil on a piece of paper resting on his sabretache and read it to Lord Raglan, who dictated some additional words.

This was the 'fourth order' issued to Lord Lucan on the day of Balaclava – the order which resulted in the Charge of the Light Brigade – and the original still exists. The paper is of poor quality, thin and creased, the lines are hurriedly written in pencil and the flimsy sheet has a curiously insignificant and shabby appearance. The wording of the order runs: 'Lord Raglan wishes the cavalry to advance rapidly to the front – follow the enemy and try to prevent the enemy carrying away the guns. Troop Horse Artillery may accompany. French cavalry is on your left. Immediate. (Sgd.) Airey.'

Captain Thomas Leslie, a member of the family of Leslie of Glaslough, was the next aide-de-camp for duty, and the order had been placed in his hand when Nolan intervened. The honour of carrying the order he claimed was his, by virtue of his superior rank and consummate horsemanship. The only road now available from the Heights to the plain 600 or 700 feet below was little more than a track down the face of a precipice, and speed was of vital importance. Lord Raglan gave way and Nolan, snatching the paper out of Captain Leslie's hand, galloped off. Just as Nolan was about to descend, Lord Raglan called out to him, 'Tell Lord Lucan the cavalry is to attack immediately.' Nolan plunged over the verge of the Heights at breakneck speed.

ANY other horseman would have picked his way with care down that rough, precipitous slope, but Nolan spurred his horse, and up on the Heights the watchers held their breath as, slithering, scrambling, stumbling, he rushed down to the plain.

So far the day had been a terrible one for Edward Nolan; even its sole glory, the charge of the Heavy Brigade, had been gall and wormwood to his soul. He was a light-cavalryman, believing passionately in the superior efficiency of light over heavy horsemen – 'so unwieldy, so encumbered', he had written – and in this, the first cavalry action of the campaign, the light cavalry had done absolutely nothing. Hour after hour, in an agony of impatience, he had watched the Light Cavalry Brigade standing by, motionless, inglorious and, as onlookers had not scrupled to say, shamefully inactive.

For this he furiously blamed Lord Lucan, as he had furiously blamed Lord Lucan on every other occasion when the cavalry had been kept out of action, 'raging', in William Howard Russell's phrase, against him all over the camp. Irish-Italian, excitable, headstrong, recklessly courageous, Nolan was beside himself with irritation and anger as he swooped like an avenging angel from the Heights, bearing the order which would force the man he detested and despised to attack at last.

With a sigh of relief the watchers saw him arrive safely, gallop furiously across the plain and, with his horse trembling, sweating and blown from the wild descent, hand the order to Lord Lucan sitting in the saddle between his two brigades. Lucan opened and read it.

The order appeared to him to be utterly obscure. Lord Raglan and General Airey had forgotten that they were looking down from 600 feet. Not only could they survey the whole action, but the inequalities of the plain disappeared when viewed from above. Lucan from his position could see nothing; inequalities of the ground concealed the activity round the redoubts, no single enemy soldier was in sight, nor had he any picture of the movements of the enemy in his mind's eye, because he had unaccountably neglected to take any steps to acquaint himself with the Russian dispositions. He should, after receiving the third order, have made it his business to make some form of reconnaissance; he should, when he found he could see nothing from his position, have shifted his ground – but he did not.

He read the order 'carefully', with the fussy deliberateness which maddened his staff, while Nolan quivered with impatience at his side. It seemed to Lord Lucan that the order was not only obscure but absurd: artillery was to be attacked by cavalry; infantry support was not mentioned; it was elementary that cavalry charging artillery in such circumstances must be annihilated. In his own account of these fatal moments Lucan says that he 'hesitated and urged the uselessness of such an attack and the dangers attending it'; but Nolan, almost insane with impatience, cut him short and 'in a most authoritative tone' repeated the final message he had been given on the Heights: 'Lord

Raglan's orders are that the cavalry are to attack immediately.'

For such a tone to be used by an aide-de-camp to a Lieutenant-General was unheard of; moreover, Lord Lucan was perfectly aware that Nolan detested him and habitually abused him. It would have been asking a very great deal of any man to keep his temper in such circumstances, and Lord Lucan's temper was violent. He could see nothing, 'neither enemy nor guns being in sight,' he wrote, nor did he in the least understand what the order meant. It was said later that Lord Raglan intended the third and fourth orders to be read together, and that the instruction in the third order to advance and recover the Heights made it clear that the guns mentioned in the fourth order must be on those Heights. Lord Lucan, however, read the two orders separately. He turned angrily on Nolan, 'Attack, sir? Attack what? What guns, sir?'

The crucial moment had arrived. Nolan threw back his head, and, 'in a most disrespectful and significant manner', flung out his arm and, with a furious gesture, pointed, not to the Causeway Heights and the redoubts with the captured British guns, but to the end of the North Valley, where the Russian cavalry routed by the Heavy Brigade were now established with their guns in front of them. 'There, my lord, is your enemy, there are your guns,' he said, and with those words and that gesture the doom of the Light Brigade was sealed.

What did Nolan mean? It has been maintained that his gesture was merely a taunt, that he had no intention of indicating any direction, and that Lord Lucan, carried away by rage, read a meaning into his out-flung arm which was never there.

The truth will never be known, because a few minutes later Nolan was killed, but his behaviour in that short interval indicates that he did believe the attack was to be down the North Valley and on those guns with which the Russian cavalry routed by the Heavy Brigade had been allowed to retire.

It is not difficult to account for such a mistake. Nolan, the cavalry enthusiast and a cavalry commander of talent, was well aware that a magnificent opportunity had been lost when the Light Brigade failed to pursue after the charge of the Heavies. It was, indeed, the outstanding, the flagrant error of the day, and he must have watched with fury and despair as the routed Russians were suffered to withdraw in safety with the much-desired trophies, their guns. When he received the fourth order he was almost off his head with excitement and impatience, and he misread it. He leapt to the joyful conclusion that at last vengeance was to be taken on those Russians who had been suffered to escape. He had not carried the third order, and read by itself the wording of the fourth was ambiguous. Moreover, Lord Raglan's last words to him, 'Tell Lord Lucan that the cavalry is to attack immediately', were fatally lacking in precision.

And so he plunged down the Heights and with a contemptuous gesture, scorning the man who in his opinion was responsible for the wretched mishandling of the cavalry, he pointed down the North Valley. 'There my Lord, is your enemy; there are your guns.'

Lord Lucan felt himself to be in a hideous dilemma. His resentment against Lord Raglan was indescribable; the orders he had received during the battle had been, in his opinion, not only idiotic and ambiguous, but insulting. He had been treated, he wrote later, like a subaltern. He had been peremptorily ordered out of his first position – the excellent position chosen in conjunction with Sir Colin Campbell – consequently after the charge of the Heavies there had been no pursuit. He had received without explanation a vague order to wait for infantry. What infantry? Now came this latest order to take his division and charge to certain death. Throughout the campaign he had had bitter experience of orders from Lord Raglan, and now he foresaw ruin; but he was helpless. The Queen's Regulations laid down that 'all orders sent by aides-de-camp . . . are to be obeyed with the same readiness, as if delivered personally by the general officers to whom such aides are attached'. The Duke of Wellington himself had laid this down. Had Lord Lucan refused to execute an order brought by a member of the Headquarters staff and delivered with every assumption of authority he would, in his own words, have had no choice but 'to blow his brains out'.

Nolan's manner had been so obviously insolent that observers thought he would be placed under arrest. Lord Lucan, however, merely shrugged his shoulders and, turning his back on Nolan, trotted off alone, to where Lord Cardigan was sitting in front of the Light Brigade.

Nolan then rode over to his friend Captain Morris, who was sitting in his saddle in front of the 17th Lancers – the same Captain Morris who had urged Lord Cardigan to pursue earlier in the day – and received permission to ride beside him in the charge.

There was now a pause of several minutes, and it is almost impossible to believe that Nolan, sitting beside his close friend and sympathizer, did not disclose the objective of the charge. If Nolan had believed the attack was to be on the Causeway Heights and the redoubts, he must surely have told Captain Morris. Morris, however, who survived the charge though desperately wounded, believed the attack was to be on the guns at the end of the North Valley.

Meanwhile Lord Lucan, almost for the first time, was speaking directly and personally to Lord Cardigan. Had the two men not detested each other so bitterly, had they been able to examine the order together and discuss its meaning, the Light Brigade might have been saved. Alas, thirty years of hatred could not be bridged; each, however, observed perfect military courtesy. Holding the order in his hand, Lord Lucan informed Lord Cardigan of the contents and ordered him to advance down the North Valley with the Light Brigade, while he himself followed in support with the Heavy Brigade.

Lord Cardigan now took an astonishing step. Much as he hated the man before him, rigid as were his ideas of military etiquette, he remonstrated with his superior officer. Bringing down his sword in salute he said, 'Certainly, sir; but allow me to point out to you that the Russians have a battery in the valley on our front, and batteries and riflemen on both sides.'

Lord Lucan once more shrugged his shoulders. 'I know it,' he said; 'but Lord Raglan will have it. We have no choice but to obey.' Lord Cardigan made no further comment, but saluted again. Lord Lucan then instructed him to 'advance very steadily and keep his men well in hand'. Lord Cardigan saluted once more, wheeled his horse and rode over to his second-in-command, Lord George Paget, remarking aloud to himself as he did so, 'Well, here goes the last of the Brudenells.'

PART TWO

COMMUNICATION SKILLS

4

EFFECTIVE SPEAKING

'Speak properly, and in as few words as you can,
but always plainly; for the end of speech is not
ostentation, but to be understood.'
William Penn, reformer and founder of Pennsylvania

Occasions for public speaking abound. In our working lives we may have to give briefings or talks, take part in presentations or even deliver formal lectures. Some occupations – notably law, politics and education – make heavy demands on the speaking abilities of their members. Others, including the managerial and supervisory professions, are beginning to share this characteristic as the art of communication becomes ever more essential for getting results through working with people.

In industry, commerce and the public services, however, the occasions for public speaking may be less formal – a few words before a meeting, a question to a committee or a briefing to initiate a special job – but these times call for effective speech from the manager or leader.

Nor should the scope of this chapter be limited entirely to the world of work. Most of us live in communities; all of us belong to families or have friends. We may never launch a ship or open a bazaar but few of us can avoid being asked 'to say a few words' at some stage or another in our lives. Our words may enhance the occasion, like a good speech at a wedding. Or our contribution may sway a meeting of a society or neighbourhood association. At work and in the local community the ability to communicate or speak well is inextricably bound up with good leadership and good membership.

THE SEARCH FOR RULES

So important is public speaking that it would be surprising if a great deal of ink had not been spilt on the subject. The earliest writer on 'rhetoric', or the art of using language so as to instruct, move or delight others, is said to have been a Sicilian called Corax in the 460s B.C. Unfortunately his treatise has not survived. In the following centuries, such practitioners as Demosthenes in Athens and Cicero in Rome brought 'rhetoric' to a high pitch of excellence according to the standards and expectations of their day. A study of their 'word skills' and writings, along with the efforts of the smaller fry of professional orators, formed the basis for later attempts at formulating the rules of 'the art of persuasion', as the Greek philosopher Aristotle called it in his own book – *Rhetoric*, written in the fourth century B.C.

Perhaps the best way to get the flavour of this passionate search for rules is to take the most complete account of the art of oratory as our framework – Quintilian's *Institutio Oratoria*, written about 95 A.D., when the Roman Empire was nearing its zenith. Like Caesar with his commentaries on Gaul and the Gallic War, the Roman rhetorician Quintilian found his subject to be divided into three parts: the art of rhetoric, the speech itself and the situation that calls it forth.

Quintilian gave most attention to 'the art of rhetoric', which in turn he placed in five divisions. The first two he called 'invention' (collecting the material) and 'disposition' (arranging it in order). Thirdly came the labour of putting it all into words, fourthly memorizing it, and finally, delivering the finished speech. The speech itself should also have five phases: an introduction to gain the goodwill of the audience; a statement of the point at issue; arguments to prove your case; refutations of contrary arguments; and then a conclusion (peroration) which either recapitulated the main points or else appealed to the audience's emotions.

It was the third part of the art of rhetoric, the putting it into words, which received the most attention from Quintilian and other writers. They called this 'elocution', from the Latin verb 'to speak out'. For the Romans this meant roughly the same as our word 'style': only later did it arrive at its modern use, which virtually limits it to pronunciation. Style covered all the skills and tricks of constructing phrases and sentences so as to serve the content in hand and please the audience.

From the earliest times we can trace the tension between content and method, the Lion and the Unicorn of language, in the disputes of the rhetoricians. One school, termed the 'Asians', favoured a flowery and elaborate style, with plenty of verbal fireworks thrown in for fun. The other school, termed the 'Atticists', advocated a plain and unadorned 'elocution'. Allowing the content to speak for itself, they frowned on unnecessary frills. In architecture we may trace the same developments made visible: the ornate splendours of Baroque on the one hand, contrasting with the more austere line and proportion of classic Greek and Roman buildings on the other.

Demosthenes never added stylistic ornaments to embellish his own speeches but he kept the audience on the edge of their seats with a variety of devices: paradoxical arguments, dramatic outbursts, imaginary dialogues, the repetition of salient points and a wit that could be crude, scurrilous and bitter. But his language was simple, at times colloquial. Cicero, almost two centuries later, blended the Atticist and Asian approaches. He was a master of the long, rolling, 'periodic' sentences, which he could break out upon the shores of his audiences' minds. When he was summoning up anger against his political opponents his sentences could sound clipped and staccato, like arrows rattling ferociously on a shield. While Cicero never lost sight of the immediate essential – the point he wanted to make – he could align words with such a fine ear that they sounded like poetry. Indeed, we are told that on occasion, when he uttered a particular combination of syllables at the end of a sentence, the audience would leap to their feet in tumultuous applause.

By considering the third and last general category in Quintilian's treatise – the kind of speech – we can see the weakness in this whole attempt to construct a science of rhetoric or oratory. Quintilian recognized three main types of speech to which his rules would apply: show speeches (which he called 'demonstrative' ones), political or 'deliberative' ones, and legal pleadings. We only have to reflect on arguably one of the most influential speeches of all time – the Sermon on the Mount as depicted in the Gospel of St. Matthew – delivered not a dozen years before Quintilian's birth, and one that does not fit any of these categories, to realize how many kinds of speaking are left out of the traditional classification.

As the centuries passed these limitations became more apparent. Rhetoric became backward-looking; it ossified by failing to adapt to the changing situation and the consequent needs of practical men. From politics and public life the concept of rhetoric retreated into the law courts and academies. It became increasingly identified with form (or methods) rather than content; with the mannerisms of speech and gesture that we owe more to the Asians than the Atticists.

Not only the kinds of speeches but also the audiences changed and these alterations rendered the more static corpus of books on rhetoric out of date. The same is true for modern manuals on public speaking in our own dynamic world. Even Winston Churchill's oratory, much of which was delivered less than a hundred years ago and most between 1939 and 1945 during the Second World War, now sounds a little dated.

Yet the thoughts of the Greek and Roman masters on the six elements of human communication – the points and centre of the Communication Star described in Chapter 2 (see 'The Communication Star' diagram on page 20) – are well worth attending to.

For example, these orators never saw public speaking as a mere string of techniques, gimmicks or tricks of persuasion. They focused attention upon the moral as well as the intellectual and educational gifts of the communicator. As the Roman statesman Cato said, a true orator is 'a good man skilled in speaking'. This certainly rings true with Quintilian, whose integrity and kindliness still shine through the pages of his treatise.

Secondly, the Greek and Roman masters were aware of the importance of the content: they knew that truth or justice communicates better than lies or evil. Of course they knew also that a skilful speaker could cause an untruth or injustice to be accepted, and some believed that the good of the state sometimes justified such advocacy. But they recognized this as being in some ways an inversion of the natural order. Values such as goodness, happiness, justice and moderation were the 'places' where arguments could be found.

The word 'topics' – the Greek word for 'places' – was used by Aristotle in the same way and is still used today.

Thirdly, the traditional theorists of ancient times stressed the advantages of 'knowing' your audience and this remains equally valid in modern times. These theorists were especially interested in the psychology of emotions such as anger or pity. At this point in the twenty-first century – having witnessed the negative effects of emotion-arousing oratory as demonstrated by Hitler and Mussolini, for example – we are in a cultural phase where many people tend to distrust or shy away from emotional displays. Thus, this aspect of 'knowing' people may not greatly appeal to us. But it is the abiding message of the past great oratorial masters that a thorough knowledge of people in general – and the audience in particular – is essential if the aims of public speaking are to be achieved. In the terse words of Cicero these aims are *docere, movere, delectare:* to instruct, to move and to delight.

FIVE PRINCIPLES OF GOOD SPEAKING – AND COMMUNICATION

Should we abandon the search for principles or rules and rely upon the mind's general thinking abilities of analysing, synthesizing and valuing in order to be good oral communicators? There are two reasons why I do not think so.

Firstly, the gap between our mind's general faculties and the highly specific actual situations of speaking aloud to one or more people is too wide: we need some bridges across it, some ready-made shapes into which these abilities can flow. Merely to tell someone to analyse (content, audience and situation) and synthesize (content with methods) is not enough. Such advice would be too general.

Secondly, although each communication is unique –

unlike any before or after – to some extent they can be grouped into families. The wedding speech situation has a habit of cropping up repeatedly, for example, as do election or leaving speech situations. Thus it should be possible to make some generalizations.

But what sort of generalizations and can we apply rules to sort them? Rules themselves come in assorted sizes and shapes. 'Love your neighbour' is qualitatively different from 'Brush your teeth after meals'. The danger of being too specific is that you ignore the situational variables. The rule then has the advantage of being concrete and practical but it accumulates a 'tail' of 'ifs' and 'buts'. As the months pass it can die the proverbial death of a thousand qualifications. If, on the other hand, the rules are too general they become too abstract, and the mind cannot get a purchase on them. We may agree but we do not buy them in the auction of practical ideas. 'Think!' may be a good rule, but it does not help very much.

The answer may lie in the identification of the appropriate *values*. Values come in different galaxies and clusters. Where communication is concerned we need to be able to call into play a certain family of values, so that they intermingle with the intellectual and practical work of analysing and synthesizing content, methods, communicants and situation. Values are not victims to changes in fashion or to the whims of particular situations as rules are – they last.

Now to work! I suggest that there are Five Principles of Good Speaking – BE CLEAR, BE PREPARED, BE SIMPLE, BE VIVID and BE NATURAL – but the list is open-ended. You may be able to add to the list. In order to make them easy to remember, I have set the five key principles out as exhortations or self-commands. They are what I habitually tell myself to do when about to speak – not always with good effect!

BE CLEAR

Clarity is the cardinal principle of power or effectiveness in both speech and writing. Therefore good communication begins in the mind. The French poet Nicholas Boileau expressed this truth in 1674:

> *What is conceived well is expressed clearly,*
> *And words to say it will arise with ease.*

Clear thinking issues in a clear utterance: if your thoughts or ideas are a bit confused, vague or fuzzy, then they will be that much less easily understood or perceived.

Thus the application of this principle begins a long way back from the boardroom or executive office. It begins in the struggle to achieve clarity in the uncertain weather of the mind. This entails mastering the intellectual skills of analysing, synthesizing and valuing. You can find out more about these in my companion book *Effective Decision Making*.

However, it should not be supposed that what is *clear* is automatically *true*. Someone once said that the Irish playwright George Bernard Shaw's head contained a confusion of clear ideas. Be that as it may, truth does not always come purified and translucent and 'All that glisters is not gold'.

Clarity is a mercenary value: it serves well whoever is prepared to pay the price for it. That price includes the willingness to suffer muddle, confusion and ambiguity before the clouds part, the dust settles, and the issue, problem or course of action becomes crystal-clear. If it becomes a matter of communicating to others, the combination of truth and clarity is well-nigh irresistible, certainly so in the long run.

One of the masters of our time in applying the principle of Be Clear was Field Marshal Montgomery. His wartime briefings became a legend to those who heard him. As a boy at St Paul's School in London, I heard ex-pupil Viscount Montgomery speak when he visited the school to describe his D-Day plans. He spoke in the very building that was used during the Second World War as Allied Headquarters – indeed in the same lecture room that he and the other generals used for their final presentations to King George VI and Churchill. So, it was not difficult for a fourteen-year-old boy to capture the 'atmosphere', as Montgomery liked to call it.

Above all, his refreshing clarity lingers. Brigadier Essame emphasized it in the following account of Montgomery at work in Ronald Lewin's *Montgomery as a Military Commander* (1971):

> He could describe a complex situation with amazing lucidity and sum up a long exercise without the use of a single note. He looked straight into the eyes of the audience when he spoke. He had a remarkable flair for picking out the essence of a problem, and for indicating its solution with startling clarity. It was almost impossible to misunderstand his meaning, however unpalatable it might be.

The principle of Be Clear needs to wipe away any stains or marks that discolour the work of arrangement, reasoning and expression in our minds. The arrangement or structure of what you are saying should be clear, so that people know roughly where they are and where they are going. The reasoning should be sharp and clean-cut, without the blurred edges of those who gloss over the issues. Above all, the *value* dimension of the matter in hand should be clarified, for it is this realm that releases most mud into the pools of thought. Lastly, the principle of lucidity invites us to shun the obscure reference, the clouded remark, the allusion that few will understand or the word that is fashionable but all too muddy in its meaning.

BE PREPARED

Achieving clarity about your aim, content and plan – be it for a formal presentation or an informal speech – is a key part of preparation.

Most people know the terse Scout motto 'Be Prepared'. Of course you cannot be prepared for every contingency in life, except in a general sense of having a certain mental resilience by which you can face situations not necessarily known in advance. But you can be ready for those occasions when you know you have to make a speech of some kind or another. You may have weeks or only a few minutes at your disposal but the principle of preparation is still applicable.

What manner or degree of preparation you can achieve will vary considerably but it is useful to distinguish between *general preparation* and *particular preparation*. If you are a portrait painter, for example, most if not all of your training and experience should have equipped you for the moment when you actually action a portrait, as illustrated by the case study below:

The famous portrait painter Sir Joshua Reynolds, first President of the Royal Academy, once painted the portrait of a successful iron magnate, a self-made man of immense wealth. Like many rich men he was careful with his money. When he received the invoice for some hundreds of guineas – a great sum in those days – he exploded with anger and walked over to Sir Joshua's studio to complain.

'You spent no more than twelve hours on my face,' he declared, 'and your assistants did most of the work on the rest of me. Why charge me over six hundred pounds for twelve hours' work? I wouldn't pay my best manager that sum.'

'You are not paying me for twelve hours, Sir,' replied Reynolds. 'You are paying me for over thirty years in which I learnt with much toil and trouble what to do with my brushes in those twelve hours.'

'All my life has been a preparation for loving you,' wrote the English writer G. K. Chesterton to his future wife. In the context of communication, *general preparation* reaches back to your schooldays when you learnt to read and write, to discuss and debate, to put up your hand in the class when you knew the answer. It also embraces all your subsequent learning – usually on the job – of the principles and practice of good communication. This whole book is both a summary of and a contribution to all the general preparation that has already taken place in your life.

Particular preparation covers what soldiers would call the tactics of the situation. For the portrait artist it means such activities as putting primer on the canvas, selecting and arranging the brushes and paints and making sure that the studio is warm and well lit. It may have already included some reflection on the personality or character of the sitter who is coming that day – what music they may like to listen to, what they like to talk about or what refreshments to offer them.

The equivalents before any kind of communication are set out below, using the framework of Rudyard Kipling's verse from 'The Elephant Child' in the *Just So Stories* (1902):

> *I keep six honest serving-men*
> *(They taught me all I knew);*
> *Their names are What and Why and When*
> *And How and Where and Who.*

In the table opposite I have changed their order, but it really doesn't matter which one you take first. They are like six chisels that you need to keep in your mental tool bag, always sharp and ready for service.

Time is often in short supply for preparations, but it is rare to find yourself without even a minute or two to make a plan. Such crisis occasions, I suppose, do have the advantage of revealing the person who is more or less always ready to speak in certain areas if called upon to do so. But the good communicator seeks to avoid these surprises.

One lesson I have learnt the hard way is not to become rigid or inflexible when you strive to Be Prepared. Having planned your work, the natural instinct is to work your plan. The difficulty is that plans imply some picture of what the situation is going to be like – and 'on the day' it might not be like that at all, as the case study below illustrates:

Henry Compton was incensed by the prospect of having a motorway extension through the fields next to his garden. He carefully planned and prepared what he was going to say at the public inquiry. He listed ten points as to why it would damage the natural environment, especially the habitat of a rare spotted African woodpecker that occasionally visits these shores.

Once the planning officers had outlined the proposal and the Chairman threw it open to discussion, Henry waited for an opportunity to jump in with his prepared speech, which he had timed for ten minutes.

'Owing to time pressure most of the contributions will now have to be restricted to three minutes. Mr Compton next,' someone announced.

Henry rose to his feet and launched into his ten-minute speech. By the time he had reached his third point – it all took longer than he thought – the Chairman interrupted him and he had to sit down. All Henry had managed to

BE PREPARED – SOME GUIDELINES FOR THINKING AHEAD	
KEY QUESTION	NOTES
Who?	Who are you going to communicate to? Try to visualize them – an individual, several persons or an audience. What are their interests, presuppositions and values? What do they share in common with others; how are they unique?
What?	What do you wish to communicate? One way of answering this question is to ask yourself about the 'success criteria'. How will you know if and when you have successfully communicated what you have in mind?
How?	How can you best convey your message? Language is important here. Choose your words with the audience in mind. Plan a beginning, middle and end. If time and place allow them, consider and prepare some audio-visual aids.
When?	Timing is all important in communication. Develop a sense of timing, so that your contributions are seen and heard as relevant to the issue or matter in hand. There is a time to speak and a time to be silent. 'It is better to be silent than sing a bad tune.'
Where?	What is the physical context of the communication in mind? You may have time to visit the room, for example, and rearrange the furniture. Check for audibility (and visibility if you are using visual aids).
Why?	In order to convert hearers into listeners you need to know why they should listen to you – and tell them if necessary. What disposes them to listen? This implies that you yourself know why you are seeking to communicate and know the value, worth or interest of what you are going to say.

do was to repeat what had already been said. His tenth point and ace trump – the African woodpecker – was left out in the cold.

So committed to his prepared message was Henry Compton that he was not delicately attuned to the meeting. Had he been so, he would have sensed that the numbers of people wanting to speak in a limited time frame would put a premium on hard-hitting brevity. When faced with the need for a last-minute change of plan, he couldn't cope. And so he lost his opportunity.

BE SIMPLE

Avoid giving your listeners undue difficulties. In this context *simple* refers to something that is not complicated or intricate and is therefore capable of being quickly grasped by the mind. It should not be confused with *easy*, which merely points to that which requires little effort to do.

The search for simplicity in thinking is the same as the search for the essence of a subject, that which is specific to it and not composite or mixed up with other matters. Such a quest demands skills of analysing. We have to dissect, discard, blow and burn before we isolate the essential simplicity of a subject. 'To simplify' means to render less intricate or difficult and thus capable of being more easily understood, performed or used.

Keep it simple

Former British Prime Minister Harold Macmillan once related how after his maiden speech in the Commons, his legendary predecessor David Lloyd George – one of the great political

orators of the twentieth century – asked him to come and see him. Lloyd George complimented Macmillan on his first attempt and then gave him a tip: 'If you are an ordinary Member of Parliament, make only one point in your speech (you can make it in different ways but it should centre on one point). If you are a minister, you may make two. Only if you are a Prime Minister, can you afford to make three points.'

At this point we may fruitfully distinguish between making things simple in the sense illustrated above and *over-simplification*. To Be Simple requires a lot of hard work, especially if we have to present a subject that has many complications when studied in detail. But even if the subject is inherently complex we still have the choice to make between presenting its complexities in the simplest possible way, or reflecting the complications in both the arrangement of our talk and the language we employ. The ability to speak simply about difficult subjects – without over-simplification – is one of the marks of an effective speaker. We should certainly not fall into the trap of equating simplicity with being simplistic or superficial. What is simple may have depth, just as sophistication may disguise emptiness.

EXERCISE: Being Simple
Take a little time to answer the following questions. They should help to provide some clarity on the concept of Being Simple:

- Can you think of someone in your professional field who has the gift of making complex matters sound simple without talking down or becoming simplistic?
- Choose one aspect of your work that is by universal consent not easy for a layperson to understand. How

would you explain it to a group of hunter-gatherer South American Indians through an interpreter?

- List three reasons why professional people sometimes deliberately choose to take an essentially simple subject in their field and make it sound as complicated as possible.

When Being Simple, however, it is important also to be aware of any difficulties involved and to work your way through any complexities to the heart of the matter – this is where the essential simplicity of a phenomenon lies. This is as true for the scientist as for the manager, as illustrated by the accolade below, made by Max Perutz, a Nobel Prize-winner in chemistry, about the capability of Professor Sir Lawrence Bragg, Nobel Laureate and pioneer of crystallography:

> His mind leaps like a prima ballerina, with perfect ease. What is so unique about it – and this is what made his lectures so marvellous – is the combination of penetrating logic and visual imagery. Many of his successes in crystal structure analysis are due to this power of visualizing the aesthetically and physically most satisfying way of arranging a complicated set of atoms in space and then having found it, with a triumphant smile, he would prove the beauty and essential simplicity of the final solution.

Wherever we look we find the same story: good speakers naturally apply the principle of Be Simple and it is the less good ones who lose themselves and their audience in a maze of complications, real and imagined. Former Chancellor Willy Brandt of West Germany said of Jean Monnet, the father of the Common Market: 'He had the ability to put complicated matters into simple formulae.' Doubtless in politics simplicity is a sign of statesmanship just as it accompanies outstanding ability in the arts and sciences.

Apart from content and arrangement the principle of Be Simple should also be applied to language. Here we have to fight an endless battle against the thoughtless use of jargon in public conversation or speeches. But again the price of freedom from this particular piece of professional tyranny is the knowledge of the complications and ramifications that the trade vocabulary, signs and symbols have come to stand for. Otherwise the talk will be *simpliste* – over-simple or naive. Perhaps we have to earn the right to speak simply.

'I'm allowed to use plain English because everybody knows that I could use mathematical logic if I chose,' wrote logician and philosopher Bertrand Russell in *Portraits from Memory* (1956). 'I suggest to young professors that their first work be in a jargon only to be understood by the erudite few. With that behind them, they can ever after say what they have to say in a language "understanded" of the people.' His advice applies equally well to all who have to speak to their fellow men about technical matters.

In practical matters, where the desired result of communication is action, the simpler the instructions plans the more likely people are to remember them and therefore carry them through. Writing to Lady Hamilton in October 1805 from HMS *Victory* (letter reproduced in *Nelson's Letters*, ed. G. Dawson, J. M. Dent, 1960), Lord Nelson described the reaction of his captains to the strategy he outlined for the impending Battle of Trafalgar:

I joined the Fleet late on the evening of the 28th but could not communicate with them until the next morning. I believe that my arrival was most welcome, not only to the Commander of the Fleet, but also to every individual in it; and when I came to explain to them the '*Nelson touch*', it was like an electric shock. Some shed tears, all approved – 'It was new – it was singular – it was simple!' and, from

Admirals downwards, it was repeated – 'It must succeed,
if ever they will allow us to get at them.'

BE VIVID

Nelson certainly made his battle plan vivid. Oddly enough,
he avoided giving speeches or making addresses, which
suggests that he was no public speaker. He was, however, a
most effective communicator to his captains and crews. He
could give even a naval strategy visual impact and dramatic
appeal. Could you do the same to next year's marketing
plan?

The principle of vividness covers all that goes to make
what we say interesting, arresting and attractive. From the
Latin verb *vivere* meaning 'to live', the word vivid literally
translates as 'full of life'. The characteristics it points to
spring from the presence of young kicking life in both the
speaker (whatever his or her age) and the subject: vigorous,
active, enthusiastic, energetic, strong, warm, fresh, bright,
brilliant and lively. When the subject or content is clear and
simple it is already well on the road to becoming vivid but
we may still have to let it come to life.

Thus vividness is not something that can be lightly super-
imposed when all the other preparatory work is completed.
Nor is it the result of giving one's personality full play to
express itself, like a fountain playing in the sunlight. All
public speaking, however slight the occasion, should be 'truth
through personality'. It is the truth that we have to vivify or
bring to life for the other person, never ourselves. Only then
can the speaker produce what the English poet Thomas Gray
called 'thoughts that breathe, and words that burn'.

The first application of the principle Be Vivid is to be
interested in what you are talking about and the persons to

whom you are talking to – in that order. Interest, one of the forms of life itself, is a magnetic quality that is found in people but not in subjects. It is true, of course, that genetic inheritance, family upbringing and education pre-dispose us to being interested in certain subjects or topics rather than others. But these fields are as broad as the plains: people, things, ideas, the past, present or future. Within such expanses there are many camping grounds. Moreover, we share some common or universal traits, and if one human person is genuinely interested in some subject it will be surprising if he can find no one to share his interest.

Interest, however, can be a quiet and unassuming move-ment of the mind. We may acknowledge it in others, but not be necessarily moved to share it. Not all those who have an interest in what they wish to communicate also possess the gift of kindling interest in an audience. But we all find it hard to resist enthusiasm, which is interest blazing and crackling with happy flames. It is extremely difficult for an enthusiastic speaker to be dull: quite naturally he or she is applying the principle of Being Vivid.

On enthusiasm – the life-giver

Enthusiasm consists of a permanent intense delight in what is happening in the life around us at all times, combined with a passionate determination to create something from it, some order, some pattern, some artefacts, with gusto and delight. It means attacking problems, puzzles and obstacles with gump-tion and with relish.

We can develop this drive in ourselves by consciously looking for the enthralling, the exciting, the enchanting, the emotionally moving in even the most routine or most trivial matters, and applying ourselves to it with all the vigour of which we are capable. We don't have to display a frenzy of histrionics and so become a menace to our friends. But we do need to enjoy unashamedly and uninhibitedly whatever we are doing.

John Casson, 'Are You Getting Through?', *Industrial Society*, November 1970

Beyond these essentials quite how you apply the principle of vividness depends upon your creative imagination. Where mass communications are involved, a theatrical sense for the 'drama' may be the way forward. Montgomery and Nelson both 'stage-managed' their communications. 'Monty', alone on the stage, tiers of coloured medal ribbons on his battle-dress, could communicate the inherent drama of battle. Nor was it perhaps just chance that Nelson loved a former actress, or that he insisted on donning his dress uniform of blue laced with gold on the fateful day of Trafalgar. Above all, he had the ability to capture a great moment and let it speak for itself, with all the flair of a great actor on the stage.

In smaller gatherings or groups and in less intrinsically dramatic situations the attempt to be dramatic can soon land us on the rocks of amateur theatricals. Thus the first step is always to look for *relevant* vividness in the subject. For example, I recall one afternoon's instruction in the army on digging trenches. After a talk on the theory of it, we recruits were marched to the middle of a large field, given spades and told that in thirty minutes a machine-gun would sweep the field with fire. None of us had ever dug so fast in our lives ... It was a lesson on a seemingly humdrum subject – that of digging a trench – but the instructor had discovered and released the vividness within it.

One way to heighten speech or give it more dramatic impact is to use the colouring of metaphor or analogy. But remember that language should serve meaning, as method should serve content. For both meaning and content are always constantly in danger of 'take-over' bids from language and methods, such as metaphors or visual aids. The test is always the practical one: do people get the message or do they only chuckle over the vivid analogy or colourful visual aid, the illustrative story or the memorable phrase? Demosthenes, by acclaim the greatest of Athenian orators and a prominent political leader in the long struggle against the encroachments of King Philip of Macedon, once said to a rival: 'You make the audience say, "How well he speaks!" I make them say, "Let us march against Philip!"'

Pictures bring vividness, be they actual or verbal. The visual metaphor or simile is a short and vivid picture, which also aids clarity and simplicity. Humour can also enliven working communications, for laughter and boredom cannot live long together. Communication can be a serious business, but it need rarely be a solemn one. Just remember not to let vividness of image or humour draw attention away from the message.

BE NATURAL

To a large extent the previous four principles can be applied before a talk or speech begins, even though there are only a few minutes to consider what you are going to say and how you will put it. The fifth principle of Be Natural belongs primarily to the stage of delivery: it governs our manner of speaking. Of course it can also influence all our preliminary thinking, for both the subject and the methods chosen should be natural to you, or have become so.

Effortless grace

Many things – such as loving, going to sleep or behaving unaffectedly – are done worst when we try hardest to do them.

         C. S. Lewis, *Studies in Medieval and Renaissance*
                                          Literature

When it comes to public speaking, art – like all grace – should not destroy nature but perfect it. Here situational influences can be especially troublesome. We all know how difficult it can be to act naturally in certain circumstances. We should think nothing of jumping a four-foot-wide stream but a similar gap several thousand feet up on a mountain cliff can make us freeze with nerves. The principle of Be Natural' invites you to shut off the danger signals from the situation and speak as naturally as if you were standing in your own room at home. Easier said than done. Yet the art of relaxing can help to fight off the strained voice. The natural and relaxed manners of experienced television entertainers give us plenty of models for observation.

The principle of naturalness is not, however, a licence to be your own worst self before a captive audience. Relaxation can so easily slip into sloppiness, just as 'doing what comes naturally' may be sometimes rightly interpreted by the audience as an inconsiderate lack of adequate preparation. Nor should friendly mumbling or inconsequential chatter, laced with 'you knows', be mistaken for naturalness. The principles must be taken together. Speaking distinctly is the principle of Be Clear applied to the actual activity of speaking: it is our ordinary natural speech magnified to meet the larger situation.

Many of the textbooks on communication devote much

space to the techniques of breathing, intonation, pronunciation and gesturing. Doubtless there is much to be learnt
here but it is possible to overstress the importance of these
elocutionary actions. Beyond the essentials of clear and
distinct speech there is little that must be said. Variety in
tone and pitch stem from one's natural interest and enthusiasm. If they are 'put on' or practised in front of the mirror,
the result can seem self-conscious and even theatrical – in a
word, unnatural.

Being natural should not be equated with vocal relaxation.
It includes giving expression in our speech to the natural
emotions that human flesh is heir to. For many of us, our
education and culture teach us to suppress any public display
of emotion and this can make communication sound stilted
and artificial. It is unfashionable for orators to weep in
public nowadays, although Churchill brushed the odd tear
from his eye on more than one occasion. But naturalness
follows if we allow the emotions of the moment – interest,
curiosity, anger or passion – to colour our voices and
movements. Yet they should serve the voice and not master
it. 'I act best when my heart is warm and my head cool,'
declared the US actor Joseph Jefferson, a sound principle for
anyone who speaks to an audience.

If clarity, simplicity and vividness describe the *quality* of
what you say, and truth, beauty and goodness determine the
value of what you say, conciseness is about the *quantity* dimension. Essentially conciseness means brevity of expression. In
an age conscious of the value of time – 'time is money', as
US Founding Father Benjamin Franklin said – and of time
management, long-windedness is a short-cut to losing the
interest of colleagues as well as customers or clients.

Your ability to confine weighty matters to a relatively
small space in time calls for almost surgical skills of thought.
As the Arab proverb says, 'Measure the cloth seven times

before you cut your coat.' The Latin verb *concidere* meaning 'to cut short' lies behind the word 'concise'. You have to cut out all that is superfluous or elaborative when you speak. Aim at the ideal of using exactly as many words as are required to express what you have in mind – and no more.

CHECKLIST:
PUTTING THE PRINCIPLES OF COMMUNICATION TO WORK

	Yes	No
'You win the match before you run onto the field.' Do you believe this sporting maxim applies to speaking?	☐	☐
Do you take time to plan what you are going to say before and during meetings, interviews and telephone calls?	☐	☐
Has anyone found anything you have said or written in the last week to be lacking in clarity?	☐	☐
Have you taken steps to become a clear thinker?	☐	☐
Which of these statements better describes you:		
'He/she can make the complicated sound simple.'?	☐	☐
'He/she tends to turn even the simplest matter into something that is difficult and complicated.'?	☐	☐
Are you an enthusiastic, interesting and lively speaker? (Tick No box if the following words have been used about you, or anything you have said or written, in the last year: *dull, boring, lifeless, lacking creative spark, monotonous, flat* or *pedestrian*.)	☐	☐
Do you find it difficult to relax and be yourself when you are communicating?	☐	☐
Have you a reputation for making concise oral contributions and writing succinct letters or memos?	☐	☐
Do you find that you are beginning to enjoy the art of communication?	☐	☐

KEY POINTS: EFFECTIVE SPEAKING

- Speaking takes many different forms, ranging from the formal – addresses, discourses, orations, lectures, homilies, sermons, presentations – to the less formal. The Five Principles of Good Speaking apply to them all: govern the art or power of communicating or expressing thought through the spoken word. Apply them and you will become an effective speaker.

- **BE CLEAR** makes your communication unclouded or transparent. A clear sky is one free of clouds, mists and haze. With reference to speech it means freedom from any confusion and hence easy to understand. Being clear is not primarily a matter of sentences and words. The value of clarity is an inner one: it should act as a principle, purifying thought at its source, in the mind.

- **BE PREPARED** means active, conscious deliberation and effort before action. To be unprepared, by contrast, means that you have not thought or made any attempt at readying yourself for what you know you may or will have to face. You are like a football team that never trains or plans before its matches.

- **BE SIMPLE** so that your hearers are not put off by the unnecessarily complicated or intricate. But don't over-simplify or talk down to your audience – even if they are children.

- **BE VIVID** – make it come alive! This graphic or colour quality springs from the interest and enthusiasm in the mind and heart of the communicator. But it has to become visible in your language.

- **BE NATURAL** or, if you prefer it, be yourself. What you say and how you say it should reflect your own innate character. For good communication is truth through personality.

Anything that can be said can be said clearly.
Ludwig Wittgenstein, Austrian-British logician

5

THE ART OF LISTENING

'LORD CHIEF JUSTICE:
You hear not what I say to you.

FALSTAFF:
Very well, my Lord, very well; rather an't please
you, it is the disease of not listening, the malady
of not marking, that I am troubled withal.'
William Shakespeare, Henry IV

The objective of this chapter is to help you to become a better listener. Listening has been variously called the neglected art or the forgotten skill in communication. It was in my mind a few years ago to write a book on it and I remember the reaction of a business publisher. 'Listening? No, no. That's "motherhood" stuff. Everyone thinks listening is a good thing but it confers no benefits. Our bestsellers all have clear and direct benefits to the reader or their business. Look at our titles – they are all practical, how-to-do-it manuals with a bottom line pay off.'

Well, I suppose I must have listened to him in the sense of heeding his advice, because I never wrote that book. Now I shall practise what I teach about being concise, and condense what is known about the skills of effective listening into just one chapter!

THE ART OF LISTENING

Epictetus, a Greek slave at Rome in the first century, eventually acquired his freedom and began to teach philosophy to those attracted to him, as the passage below from *The Golden Sayings of Epictetus*, ed. H. Crossley (1909) illustrates:

> 'Epictetus, I have often come desiring to hear you speak, and you have never given me an answer; now if possible, I entreat you, say something to me.'
>
> 'Is there, do you think,' replied Epictetus, 'an *art* of speaking as of other things, if it is to be done skilfully and with profit to the hearer?'
>
> 'Yes.'
>
> 'And are all profited by what they hear, or only some among them? So that it seems there is an art of listening as well as of speaking . . . To make a statue needs skill: to view a statue aright needs skill also.'

It's almost odd to describe listening as a skill. This suggests to me a set of techniques that can be learnt or acquired. There are a few techniques but they are relatively unimportant. To listen means to hear with thoughtful attention. It is to pay heed to the speaker and to what he or she is saying: careful, alert, watchful and mindful. If you think that sounds easy, remember the Turkish proverb: 'Listening requires more intelligence than speaking.'

If you want to become a better listener, it follows that you may have to radically review your whole approach to life and other people. Is it worth it? Perhaps I should take a leaf out of that publisher's book and start with the benefits.

THE BENEFITS OF BEING A BETTER LISTENER

What desirable good does this comparatively rare ability to listen give you? How does it promote your wellbeing? As the key to your motivation to improve may lie in giving you reasons for so doing, let me underline some of the advantages.

Listening is a principal way of learning

As the inventor Sir Clive Sinclair once said, 'There are bucketfuls of ideas lying around.' What is lacking is listening ears and, it must be added, the entrepreneurial skills needed to bring these ideas to market. Listen for ideas and new information at all times!

Portrait of a tycoon – Lord Roy Thomson of Fleet

His ability to concentrate was formidable. He would bend the better eye closely upon the sheets of some set of accounts, seven inches from his face, and peer into the heart of a business: generally one he contemplated buying. Figures and statistics were his main, but by no means his sole, guide to a business performance. A very nimble-witted Scottish accountant said that he had never met anyone who could sum a column of figures faster than he could himself until he met Roy. Moreover, he never forgot facts and figures. He seemed to know more about figures than accountants, just as he seemed to know more about law than lawyers ... To all that poured into the pin-holes of his narrowed vision there was to be added a verbal agility of wit and response. He was not one of your silent tycoons, hearing words and feeling no requirement to acknowledge them. Nobody ever spoke to him without getting not only an answer but a supplementary, a development of the theme, and perhaps some well-timed jocularity as well.

In the same way, he was never interviewed by anyone who could match him in the eliciting of information. His interest was in the hope that the companion might add information to some current concern, or even reveal some world which Roy had not so far entered. One of the best-known women journalists in the United States spent some fascinated hours with him, and said: 'You can say I found him disarming in his simplicity ... I was totally unprepared for his childlike curiosity about everything. He is full of questions on every imaginable subject. He pumps everyone dry which is enormously flattering. Small wonder he knows something about everything.'

> Commemorative article by the editor of *The Times*, one of the newspapers owned by Roy Thomson

---

We take in information and ideas mainly through two organs: our eyes and our ears. In reading these words at the moment you are exercising the first of these two faculties.

Books, papers and screens – forms of communication that you can read or scan – seem at first to be far superior methods of receiving information or ideas than listening. Reasons for this conclusion include:

- A listener is often one among others but when you read a book you do so on your own.
- You can turn back a page or two and re-read; it is often inconvenient or impossible to ask speakers to repeat themselves.

But there are advantages that go with receiving information or ideas through listening as opposed to reading. A knowledgeable talker, for example, will often select facts in order to condense and consolidate their information as they speak, in an effort to give you the essence of it. Writers of books, alas, are not always so economical.

Most people, as they talk, learn from the feedback of their listeners' reactions and modify their spoken words accordingly. A talker, for example, may repeat or rephrase what he or she is saying if you as the listener or the audience look puzzled. That kind of flexibility is not so easily established between a writer and a reader.

Despite what I said above about the practical difficulties of asking speakers, lecturers or broadcasters to repeat a point, in one-to-one conversations or meetings of small groups you usually do have the opportunity for on-the-spot questions of clarification. Readers seldom have opportunities to question writers – or if they do it can be a lengthy process.

Lastly, through listening we can often obtain information that is not written down. There may have been no time to do so, or the person concerned may lack the motivation and skill to commit what they know to paper.

'Every person is my superior in some way,' wrote Ralph Waldo Emerson, US essayist and philosopher, 'in that I learn from him or her.' Each person you meet is a potential teacher, if only you can find out what they have to teach. Nor will they charge you a fee. Even a bore can teach you something – patience.

Always keep a pocketbook or some paper at hand so that you can take some notes of any new ideas or information. The master thinker knows that ideas are elusive and often quickly forgotten, so he pins them down with pencil and paper. Heed the Chinese proverb: 'The strongest memory is weaker than the palest ink.'

Listening is a way of helping people

Listening to others for ideas and information is self-interested. Almost everyone has some sort of information that can be useful or relevant to you, perhaps at some later time if not now. As for ideas – especially new ideas or seminal thoughts – several hundred oysters may yield only one small lustrous white pearl but if you don't open the shells will you ever find that pearl?

There is, however, a more disinterested dimension to listening, which is to see it as a means of helping others. Professional helpers – counsellors, doctors, psychiatrists and consultants – are well aware of the human need for someone to listen, especially in those times of stress, anxiety, transition or perplexity that come upon us all as life unfolds.

In such situations we may want information or advice but more basically we need someone who will simply listen and understand as we talk about things. In today's world there is an increasing tendency to call in the professionals but such non-directive listening is the office of a friend, colleague or neighbour. Without too much effort on your part, you can do more good in this way.

But, you may say, such listening is very time-consuming. Yes, it is. I am not recommending that you write blank cheques on your time for every passer-by who hijacks your attention with their problems. You may or may not be their Good Samaritan. Remember that here, as in so many other areas, it is *quality* of listening that matters more than *quantity*. Some research suggests that if you half-listen to someone's problems they will keep coming back for more. Therefore improving your capability as a listener may actually save time for both you and the person you are listening to.

Never underestimate the good you can do by simply

listening. As the Australian pychologist Elton Mayo wrote: 'One friend, one person who is truly understanding, who takes the trouble to listen to us as we consider our problems, can change our whole outlook on the world.'

By listening you create a listener

There is a strong tendency to reciprocity or equivalence of exchange among people. You tend to receive what you give and to give what you receive. If you give listening you may receive listening. If you talk you get talk back.

Now, I know that this principle seems to contradict the complementary nature of human intercourse. The natural response to a good speaker is to listen. It's more like a party game where you take turns. If you take the part of listening while the other speaks they are much more likely to take their turn at listening while you speak with the same thoughtful attention that you have demonstrated.

'I will teach your ears to listen to me with more heed,' says Antipholus of Ephesus in Shakespeare's *The Comedy of Errors*. In planning this book I did consider putting this chapter before the preceding one on speaking. For some people, that may seem like putting the cart before the horse. Oral communication – the ability to speak well – tops the lists of essential or desirable management competencies and listening skills are seldom mentioned. But, if you think about it, the first requirement in a speaker is that they should create a listener. There is an analogy here with a business: if you cannot create and keep customers you will soon have no business. Therefore learning about listening ought logically to precede speaking.

The importance of creating a listener or an audience – not assuming them – can hardly be overstated. Musicians will tell you, for example, that the quality of listening can vary from evening to evening and that an audience who listens well can draw from the orchestra an exceptional perform-ance. As one who earns some of his living by public speaking, I can vouch for that fact from experience. One of Britain's greatest parliamentary orators, fomer Prime Minister William Pitt the Younger, once said that 'Eloquence is in the assembly, not in the speaker.'

So much for the benefits that improving your powers as a listener may bring to you. How do you do it? The first step, paradoxically, is to become more aware of what constitutes *poor* listening – in yourself as well as others.

THE DISEASE OF NOT LISTENING

People often confuse listening with hearing. But 'I hear what you say' is not the same as 'I am listening to you.' The latter implies more than reception of sounds, more even than reception of the message. It suggests the thoughtful attention and openness to the implications of what is being said that we have already been exploring.

Shakespeare in *Henry IV* makes the difference clear in a courtroom dialogue between that incorrigible old rogue Falstaff and the Lord Chief Justice, quoted at the head of this chapter.

Many of us, like Falstaff, suffer from 'the disease of not listening'. All too often listening is regarded negatively, as what you do while you are awaiting your turn to talk. Here are some of the symptoms in the syndrome of poor listening.

Selective listening

Selective listening should not be confused with listening in waves of attention, which is in fact a characteristic of the good listener. Selective listening means that you are programmed to turn a deaf ear to certain topics or themes. Adolf Hitler achieved a unique mastery in this field: he only wanted to hear good news. Those who brought him bad news, or told him the truth, encountered a glassy look and personal insult, if not worse.

The danger in selective listening is that it can become habitual and unconscious: we become totally unaware that we only want to listen to certain people or a limited range of ego-boosting news, or that we are filtering and straining information. But our friends and colleagues know fully well. And they start pre-digesting the material for us, omitting vital pieces and garnishing the rest with half-truths. And in the corridors they may mutter, 'You can't tell him the truth – he doesn't want to know.'

Your mind is like a parachute – it functions best when open.

Persistent interrupting

Persistent interrupting is the most obvious badge of the bad listener. Of course interrupting is an inevitable part of everyday conversation, springing from the fact that we can think faster than the other person can talk. So the listener can often accurately guess the end of a sentence or remark. The nuisance interrupter, however, either gets it wrong or else – even worse – he or she elbows in with a remark that shoots out the fact that they have not been listening to the half-completed capsule of meaning. They may often be working on their own next piece of talk and therefore be literally too busy to listen. Once the remark is ready, or even half-fitted, they let fly and start winding up for the next one.

Remember that even a fish would not be caught if he learned to keep his mouth shut.

Daydreaming

Daydreaming may be a natural escape from an intolerable situation, but it can also be a symptom of poor listening. It is difficult to think two things at the same time. The daydreamer has 'switched off' and his or her attention is given to an inner television screen. Some inner agenda has gained precedence over what is being said to them. The poor listener always has a monkey on his or her mental shoulder. There is a disconnected chatter going into their left inner ear – that holiday, what Mr Jones said, did I switch my car lights off, if only I was managing director I would ... Emotions can project colour pictures onto the inner screen and turn up the sound. Then – farewell to listening.

Succumbing to external distractions

Uncomfortable chairs, noise, heat or cold, sunlight or gloom: the situation can master the listener and drown the speaker and the content. The good listener will try to deal with the distraction in some helpful way; the poor one allows it to dominate their mind and rob them of attention. The higher the quality of listening the less power externals will be allowed to disrupt communication. Listening affirms or builds the relationship in the teeth of forces at work to disintegrate it. The weak listener has no extra reserves to call upon to counter such trying circumstances.

Evading the difficult or technical

Such is our addiction to the clear, simple and vivid that none of us cares for the difficult, long and dull and we throw the towel in too soon. We have a low tolerance for anything that even threatens to be difficult, coupled with an impatience at the inability of the speaker to save our time and energy by applying the principles of good speaking. But what's at issue is not merely his or her ability as a speaker but our skill as listeners. If the path has to be tortuous and uphill, the courageous listener will follow. The fainthearted or lazy listener gives up at the first obstacle.

Criticizing the speaker's delivery or visual aids

In set-piece situations such as presentations, lectures or addresses, one way of expressing one's non-listening ability is to fasten on the speaker's delivery or the quality of their audio-visual aids. Some trick of pronunciation, an accent or impediment, involuntary movements or mannerisms: all these can be seized upon as excuses for not listening to the meaning. Or the audio-visual aids, which like Hannibal's elephants can be a terror to their own side, can go on rampage and distract a weak listener. It is hard to listen when the delivery is bad and the audio-visual aids are threatening to get out of control, but such occasions do sort out the hearers from the listeners. Are you ready for your listening health check now?

CHECKLIST:
ARE YOU A BORN LISTENER YET?

	Yes	No
Do you pay close attention when others are talking?	☐	☐
When sitting next to someone you don't know at a meal do you always seek to find an area of common interest?	☐	☐
Do you believe that everyone has something to teach or share with you that has value for you – now or in the future?	☐	☐
Can you set aside such factors as a person's personality, voice or delivery in order to find out what he or she knows?	☐	☐
Are you a curious person, interested in people, ideas and things?	☐	☐
Do you respond with a smile or nod or word of encouragement as the speaker is talking? Do you maintain good eye contact?	☐	☐
Do you have a good awareness of your own prejudices, blindspots and assumptions and are you aware that they can create problems for you as a listener? Do you control them?	☐	☐
Are you patient with people who have difficulty in expressing themselves?	☐	☐
Do you keep an open mind regarding the points of view of others?	☐	☐
Do you listen for the speaker's emotional meaning as well as the subject matter content?	☐	☐
Do you often reflect, restate or paraphrase what the speaker has said in order to make sure you have the correct meaning?	☐	☐

THE SKILLS OF LISTENING

'The fact that people are born with two eyes and two ears, but only one tongue', wrote the celebrated letter writer the Marquise de Sévigné, 'suggests they ought to look and listen twice as much as they speak.' Persuading you to fall in love with listening, turning from the negative to the positive, from symptoms of disease to signs of fitness, I have summarized in the table overleaf the five skills of a good – or very good – listener. You should be able to recognize occasions when you have performed or experienced them all, so it's more a question of widening and deepening your range rather than learning something new from scratch.

In almost all instances of listening some element of *evaluation* comes in. Even if you are given a direct order by someone who has the authority to issue such orders to you, there is still a moment when you must decide whether or not to obey. If there is a moral principle at stake you may decide not to do it. If you are a soldier you may be ordered to shoot an unarmed prisoner but you ought to refuse to do so. Such occasions are mercifully rare, but the sequence of *evaluation* and *response* is happening all the time. Having grasped someone's meaning you have to assess its degree of truth. You may agree or disagree with the speaker and that will invariably influence your response. *Active listening* is quite hard mental work. Brace yourself to:

Ask questions
'He who is afraid of asking is ashamed of learning,' says one Danish proverb. Ask not only information-seeking questions but reflective ones as well, such as:

'Would it be true to say that you believe . . . ?'

SUMMARY OF LISTENING SKILLS	
Be willing to listen	The will to listening – wanting to listen – comes first. In most contexts listening also requires an openness of mind, a willingness in principle to think or act differently.
Hear the message	Receiving clearly what is actually being said – not a penny more, not a penny less – is the next vital ingredient. There may be problems in physically hearing: if so they have to be overcome. The issue at this stage is not whether or not you agree but do you hear clearly what is being said?
Interpret the meaning	The meaning in question is the speaker's meaning. It may be clear and intelligible. The test is whether or not you can play back to the other person what they mean in your own words in such a way that they accept it as accurate.
Evaluate carefully	You may want to suspend judgement so that you can use information or ideas for creative thinking purposes. But at some stage or other you will need to assess the worth or value of the content of what you have listened to. Is it true? Is it useful?
Respond appropriately	Communication is two-way. A response is called for. It may be no more than applause – or even silence. But it is still a response, which will in turn be interpreted by the speaker. Make sure you respond appropriately.

'If you had to sum up your message in one or two sentences, what would they be?'

Weigh the evidence

Assertions that such and such is the case or is true should always be examined. Some assertions may be self-evident truths but a rational person requires grounds for accepting others. What grounds for acceptance are being offered? Are they compelling or conclusive?

Watch your assumptions

We tend to make conscious or unconscious assumptions. It is difficult to think without making assumptions but the unconscious ones in particular can easily lead us into misinterpreting what the other person is saying. Jumping to conclusions – assuming that we know what someone is going to say or do – is one form it takes. Can you think of others?

You may wonder how you have time for all this critical and creative mental activity when you are busy following the sense of what is being said. A good speaker, of course, will make it easy for you to pay this kind of attention; he or she will also create some time and space for you to think by, for example, not talking too quickly.

Capitalize on thought speed

Most people talk at a speed of 125 words per minute. There is good evidence that if thoughts were measured in words per minute, most of us could think easily at about four times that rate.

The good listener uses his or her thought speed to advantage; they constantly apply their spare thinking time to what is being said. It is not difficult once one has a definite pattern of thought to follow. To develop such a pattern we should:

- Try to anticipate what a person is going to say.
- Mentally summarize what the person has been saying. What point has he made already, if any?
- Weigh the speaker's evidence by mentally questioning it.

Ask yourself, 'Am I getting the full picture, or is he or she telling me only what will prove their point?'

- Listen between the lines – the speaker doesn't always put everything that's important into words. The changing tones and volume of his or her voice may have a meaning. So may their facial expressions, the gestures they make with their hands, the movement of their bodies.

Not capitalizing on thought speed is our greatest single handicap. Yet, through listening training, this same differential can readily be converted into our greatest asset.

Ralph G. Nichols, 'How good are you at listening?', *Teamwork in Industry* (1969)

The listener should let the speaker know by verbal and/or non-verbal feedback – occasional words and nods or smiles – that the message is being received and understood. Good listeners make a point of providing such feedback in order to facilitate the communication process. The ultimate test of two-way communication, however, often lies beyond that initial response – the positive or negative. It is to be found in the realm of action: what people actually do as a consequence of the communication, not how they react. Remember that key distinction between *response* and *effect*, as shown in the case study below:

Michael Hewitt nodded enthusiastically. 'Yes, I see what you mean about always being late at handing in work and I get your point about how annoying it is to clients. It won't happen again.' Mark Wilson, the Senior Partner in the accountancy firm, felt pleased with the way Hewitt's annual performance appraisal had gone. 'At least I have sorted out that problem,' he muttered to himself. 'He really got the message this time.' But had he? Work

THE ART OF LISTENING

continued to arrive long after deadlines had expired. Not like Helen, another member of Wilson's team, who had responded so negatively to criticism about her punctuality at the appraisal interview – she even walked out of his office. But – surprise, surprise – her punctuality improved gradually but surely over the next three weeks. Michael or Helen – who had *really* received the message?

ADVANCED LISTENING

As with all arts, it is easy to make some improvements in our listening skills, but quite hard to move from satisfactory to good and even harder to progress from good to very good, while excellent eludes all but those with a special gift and special application. But we can all have the latter. We can all be excellent listeners and communicators.

'It is the heart always that sees, before the head can see,' said Thomas Carlyle, the Scottish satirical writer. A very good listener has to read 'in between the lines'. That means being able to observe and interpret any relevant non-verbal behaviour. The main categories of this undercover language have already been listed in Chapter 1 as we learn about 'The nature of communication' (page 3) but they need some explanation in this context.

A non-verbal cue, or body language, is a message – often involuntary – conveyed by such things as a speaker's eyes, posture, hand gestures, tone of voice or facial expressions. Use your eyes as well as your ears to take in information. Your unconscious or depth mind works like a computer if you will let it do so, processing all the information that you take in through the gates of the senses. The result may be those richer understandings we call intuitions.

Intuition is a way of knowing that a state exists when

there is insufficient evidence for it. The depth mind·integrates a number of pieces of data – some absorbed through our senses unconsciously – and forms an intuition that surfaces suddenly or gradually in the surface or conscious mind.

The important rule to apply to intuition is to subject those that come early to the most rigorous and sustained check. If an intuition comes only after acquiring much information or after long experience, coupled with reflection, it is much more likely to be accurate. Early intuitions are often no more than jumping to conclusions. They can be easily fed by our subterranean sources of fear and anxiety.

Empathy through listening

If a conference ... is to result in the exchange of ideas, we need to pay particular heed to our listening habits ... Living in a competitive culture, most of us are most of the time chiefly concerned with getting our own views across, and we tend to find other people's speeches a tedious interruption of the flow of our own ideas. Hence, it is necessary to emphasize that listening does not mean simply maintaining a polite silence while you are rehearsing in your mind the speech you are going to make the next time you can grab a conversational opening. Nor does listening mean waiting alertly for the flaws in the other fellow's arguments so that later you can mow him down. Listening means trying to see the problem the way the speaker sees it – which means not sympathy, which is *feeling* for him, but empathy, which is *experiencing with* him. Listening requires entering actively and imaginatively into the other fellow's situation and trying to understand a frame of reference different from your own. This is not always an easy task.

S. I. Hayakawa, author of *Language in Thought and Action* (1949)

Besides insight, or the ability to listen with a third ear as it has been called, the very good or really advanced listener is consistently going to show and use some other qualities or attributes in a rare combination: sensitivity, empathy, patience, humour, curiosity, intelligence, creativity, and – let it be added – endurance. He or she will tend to be a person of wide interests with a natural interest in people. They may be businesslike in listening but it never shows. For the essence of art is that it makes it seem natural.

Let me conclude with a verse my daughter Kate copied out and gave me when she was ten years old. It has sat in my file on 'Listening' ever since. Perhaps it was a hint!

> *A wise old owl sat in an oak,*
> *The more he heard, the less he spoke;*
> *The less he spoke, the more he heard.*
> *Why aren't we all like that wise old bird?*

KEY POINTS: THE ART OF LISTENING

- Listening is not the same as hearing. It is the positive business of paying heed or giving your thoughtful attention to someone while they are speaking.
- The benefits of becoming a good listener include information and ideas that could be profitable to you, helping others by lending them your ear, and deepening in the other person the desire to listen to you.
- As one Ghanaian proverb says: 'No one is without knowledge except he who asks no questions.'
- The first step to self-improvement is to raise your level of awareness of poor or bad listening. The symptoms of the 'disease of not listening' include irrational selectivity, irritating interruption, switching off, mental laziness,

succumbing to external distractions, and getting hung up on the speaker's voice or manner.

- Readiness to listen comes first on the list of what you need for this journey. Hearing the message clearly comes next, closely followed by the work of sifting and interpretation. That may lead to further evaluation of its content and import. You should feel responsible for giving some feedback in a conscious way, so the speaker knows if the message has been received and understood. Whether or not it further engages in your interest – or will later – is another matter.

- Listening – or at least very good listening – demands the whole of your mind and heart. That is why the challenge to become an excellent listener is such an exciting one. Not all of us may become great speakers but great listening is within our grasp.

If authority has no ears to listen, it has no head to govern.
Danish proverb

6

CLEAR WRITING

'I am looking for supreme readability. It's a
combination of lucidity, elegance and character,
so magical that many writers only pull it off once.
For the reader will hear you talking.'

A. C. Benson, British essayist and poet

For most purposes the best form of communication is the
spoken word – preferably face to face – backed up by the
written word. Say it and then confirm it in writing. Letters and
memos that are not follow-ups to oral communication – at a
meeting or over the telephone – do demand more skill from
you because they have to do all the vital work of communication
and not just a part of it. That brings us to the art of communicating through the written word – writing for short.

You should not suppose that a person who is skilled in
speaking will necessarily be a good writer, or vice versa; the
spoken and written word perform closely related but different functions. If you have ever read a transcript of a tape-
recording of a talk you have given you will see that much
revision is needed to render it into readable English. Yet it
sounded perfectly all right. Equally, famous writers are often
disappointing when they open their mouths.

Being able to set down words in writing gives us two great benefits. First, writing enables us to communicate at a distance, as when you send a letter. In pre-writing days you could, of course, send a messenger but that was doubtless expensive and also highly unreliable (witness Captain Nolan in the case study about the Charge of the Light Brigade, Chapter 3, page 38) as oral messages tend to suffer distortion in transmission. My favourite true story here concerns a prisoner-of-war camp in Italy during the Second World War, where the news that 'The Germans are in Greece' was passed from mouth to mouth and ended up as 'There is going to be a rations increase.'

The second step forward is that writing records preserves knowledge. Previously the only way that information or ideas could be preserved and handed down was by committing them to memory. Poetry and stories – myths, legends, tales, parables – both evolved because they made this labour of memory somewhat easier. The new technology of writing rendered this old technology more or less redundant, just as the introduction of the pocket calculator has made it less necessary for you or I to remember our multiplication tables off by heart.

It was no sudden revolution. The Old English word 'writan' meant 'to scratch, draw or inscribe'. The story of writing begins with man drawing, scoring or incising various surfaces such as rock faces, dried skins and clay tablets. Its high points include the evolution of alphabets, the emergence of paper and the invention of the printing press. Education, as we know it, virtually began with the necessity of teaching children – at least the children of well-to-do families – how to read and write while they were impressionable enough to acquire these complex skills. Such children enjoyed a competitive advantage in life over their illiterate fellows. Even today the abilities to read and write are the first rungs on the ladder of formal education, and – still for most people on the face of the earth – the last they will tread.

With difficulty and not by choice you have acquired the basic skill of writing. You could pick up a pen and copy out a sentence or two from this book with ease. Doubtless you write letters or emails to friends or relatives; you may use writing to store information. In this chapter I am assuming that writing is a part of your work, something that you are paid for either directly (as in my case) or indirectly. You certainly don't have to be a 'writer' by trade to include the necessity of writing letters, emails, memos, reports and possibly programmes, courses, scripts and articles in the description of your job.

Communicating on paper is an essential part of any manager's or leader's job, as indeed it is for most of us. Writing effective letters whether on paper or electronically – to customers or clients, local authorities or public bodies – is part and parcel of effective living. The art of letter writing as a social activity among friends and relatives may have been largely killed by the growth of telephoning as a means of keeping in touch but the letter for broadly business purposes still flourishes. The advent of electronic mail in particular has simply made the exchange of letters or memos much faster.

A letter is a direct or personal written, typed or printed communication, addressed to a person or organization and usually sent by post or messenger. A memo (an abbreviation of memorandum, from the Latin verb *memor* meaning 'to bring to mind') is a note to help the memory, a record of events or observations on a particular subject, especially for future consideration or use. Such information memos in business or organizational life, usually written on paper headed 'MEMORANDUM', conventionally required no signature but were often initialled by the sender.

Despite the advance of printing and transmission technology the actual business of writing an effective letter or memo comes back to your personal and professional skills as a writer. You may not think of yourself as a professional writer, but if you are in any kind of business, writing letters or memos is *part of your profession*. The aim of this chapter is to help you to become really proficient on paper so that in this respect you are more than equal to the needs of your job.

There are three elements to writing:

- Structure and layout
- Content
- Style and tone

Most of us are taught at school how to lay out a letter and structure it into paragraphs. Report writing is now also taught in the context of project work but it may present difficulties, not least because few teachers know how to write reports (I don't mean the end-of-term ones, though a brushing up of skills there would not come amiss). But it's often the case that beginners overestimate the importance of structure or layout in writing. Usually if you are clear and say what you are doing you can get away with almost anything. Conventions are important but they are relatively easy to learn and certainly are not the main thing about writing.

Content, by contrast, is literally what it is all about. Obviously I cannot advise you about content, nor can any other textbook on writing. I can help you to cook and present the dish, but the ingredients are yours alone. How the content of your written communication ultimately fares, however, will depend upon its intrinsic merits or value in that strange marketplace where truth is bought and sold.

In theory it is possible to separate content from *form* – the structure and layout plus style and tone – but in practice it is difficult to do so. Therefore you shouldn't think of style and tone as an optional extra, some pink icing on the fruit-cake but as a critical factor in communicating effectively to others. For most intents and purposes, 'the medium is part of the message'.

THE SECRET OF STYLE

Having emphasized the differences between speaking and writing it is now time to look at the other side of the coin. When you write you should think of yourself as talking directly to the person concerned. That is relatively easy if you are writing a love letter but much more difficult if you are writing to people you don't know personally. But it can be done.

Once you start to see writing as a branch of speaking and not as a separate discipline you can then apply the Five Principles of Good Speaking – Be Clear, Be Prepared, Be Simple, Be Vivid and Be Natural – that we discussed in Chapter 4 (see page 59). As you will see below, they have emerged not out of my own head but from an evolution of experience in what works in writing English. As early as the seventeenth century, for example, the first historian of the Royal Society, Thomas Sprat, mentioned the society's rejection of the 'amplifications, digressions and swellings of style' seen in contemporary writings, in favour of a 'close, natural and naked way of speaking'.

On keeping it simple

Anyone who wishes to become a good writer should endeavour, before they allow themselves to be tempted by the more showy qualities, to be direct, simple, brief, vigorous, and lucid.

This general principle may be translated into practical rules in the domain of vocabulary as follows:

- prefer the familiar word to the far-fetched
- prefer the concrete word to the abstract
- prefer the single word to the circumlocution
- prefer the short word to the long
- prefer the Saxon word to the Romance (i.e. Latin)

These rules are given roughly in order of merit; the last is also the least.

H. W. and F. G. Fowler, *The King's English* (1906)

Of course the use of short, concrete words will not in itself do the trick. The principles of clarity and simplicity have to work at the *thinking* level first and then they may produce the fruit of 'close, natural and naked' language. There are no short cuts to simplicity; this is because it is an intellectual virtue. The extract below from a *Fortune* magazine article on 'The Language of Business' further emphasizes the need for simplicity:

> Simplicity is an elusive, almost complex thing. It comes from discipline and organization of thought, intellectual courage – and many other attributes more hard won than by short words and short sentences. For plain talk – honest plain talk – is the reward of simplicity, not the means to it. The distinction may seem slight, but it is tremendously important.

The need for simplicity in language must be balanced against the first principle, which is clarity. All communication – just like sketching or painting – involves leaving some things out. The substance and aids to accuracy – stating all the relevant facts, defining terms, following logical steps – demand that certain things should be kept in, even at the expense of brevity. Over-brief or mutilated writing inevitably creates the need for further correcting communications and so nothing is gained.

The Five Principles of Good Speaking – or the Five Principles of Good Communication as we may also refer to them later is this book – should not be seen as separate or detachable guides or rules: they ought to qualify each other like checks and balances in any situation and it is all of them working together as a team that matters. Be Prepared, for example, ought to include a general knowledge of written English, distilled into such rules as 'prefer the active to the passive verb', as well as the accepted customs over spelling and punctuation. But this should be balanced by the principle Be Natural. The best writers, like the naturally good soldiers of ancient days, are those who have undergone the formal drills and manoeuvres of their discipline and then been allowed to revert to their former ferocious selves.

The winning combination

He that will write well in any tongue, must follow this counsel of Aristotle, to speak as the common people do, to think as wise men do; and so should every man understand him, and the judgement of wise men praise him.

Roger Ascham, didactic writer and tutor to Queen Elizabeth I

In today's ever-busier world, where time is at such a premium, the principle of being concise is especially important. As a manager, you are dealing explicitly in the commodities of money and time. Long letters or memos cost money in terms of secretarial wages and postal charges. Thus conciseness is an essential for the business writer. Not for you the luxury of spreading yourself over many pages. For a writer, even a letter writer, is drawing upon the precious limited time of the reader, those minutes and hours that measure out our lives. Wasting time is wasting life. Thus, above all, the manager has to aim at an accurate brevity – a concise and exact use of words – or at the economy of the reader's or hearer's attention.

In that context of management, letters, reports and emails are the main means of written communication. In the sections below I shall offer you some ideas of how to apply the Five Principles of Good Communication – Be Clear, Be Prepared, Be Simple, Be Vivid and Be Natural – in order to make your written products effective.

HOW TO WRITE A GOOD BUSINESS LETTER

As soon as you are more or less clear in your mind what you want to say in a letter, make a first draft on paper or on your word processor if you use one. The golden rule in all writing is to get something on paper or up on screen and then play about with it.

If possible, I suggest that you leave the letter for some time so that you come back to it with a fresh and objective mind. You will probably see some things you want to alter at once. The table opposite may help.

Remember to check through and correct the final draft. Then choose the appropriate form of greeting and signature. Ensure that you have attached the relevant enclosures and that you have kept a copy for your file.

STEPS IN LETTER REVISION REVISING YOUR FIRST DRAFT	
KEY AREA	**NOTES**
Objective	The objective or message of the letter should be clear. What response you expect or would like from the reader – if any – should also be clearly expressed.
Order	You may want to revise the order of your points or paragraphs within the broad parameters of BEGINNING, MIDDLE and END.
Style	Check the lengths of your paragraphs and sentences. Try reading the letter out aloud. Take out unintended repetitions. Avoid jargon.
Word selection	Cut out obscure words and clichés, as well as adverbial verbiage such as 'by and large', 'on the whole' or 'all things being equal'.
Tone	Carry out a tone check on the letter. Is it set in the right musical key? Does the tone accurately reflect your feelings? If necessary, tone down – or tone up.
Grammar/ Spelling	Lastly, check the grammar and punctuation. Avoid any spelling mistakes if possible: they may create amusement if not annoyance in the reader, distracting them from your message. Computer spellcheck and grammar tools can easily help you do this if you are writing electronically. An up-to-date dictionary is helpful if you are using pen and paper.
Layout	Does the layout look attractive? Does it sell to the eye? Word processing technology can help you to format or professionally lay out a letter using guidance or templates. Make use of these tools.

THE IMPORTANCE OF TONE

The physical conventions for setting out a business letter need not concern us here. Nor should the common sense importance of deploying a style that is lucid and clear, so that the reader is left in no doubt as to your meaning, retain us further. But the demand for economy, which I have stressed, can lead to a charge of terseness. It is vital that the *tone* of the letter should reflect your true feelings. The *Oxford English Dictionary* defines tone as 'a particular quality, pitch, modulation, or inflection of the voice expressing ... affirmation, interrogation, hesitation, decision, or some feeling or emotion'. Business letters are more likely to be effective if they are written in a tone of courtesy. Watch out for the negative viruses that can so easily infect the tone of your letters, as shown in the table opposite:

You may feel justified in sending a furious tirade to someone. But there are wiser ways to express or vent your anger, such as a workout in the gym or by digging the garden. You will at least have gained the benefit of exercise. When you have cooled down and begun to write, listen for your still-smouldering embers, like those listed above.

Courtesy – polite or respectful speech or action – is not an 'optional extra' of good style; it belongs to its very heart. Good style shows that you are at least taking the reader's interest seriously. The Cornish writer and literary critic Sir Arthur Quiller-Couch made this point in *On the Art of Writing* (1916):

Essentially style resembles good manners. It comes of endeavouring to understand others, of thinking for them rather than yourself – of thinking, that is, with the heart as well as the head ... So (says Fénelon) ... 'your words will be fewer and more effectual, and while you make less ado, what you do will be more profitable.'

SOME NEGATIVE ELEMENTS OF TONE	
Curtness	The virus of inordinate brevity communicates unconcern for your reader.
Sarcasm	Most people dislike being on the receiving end of this so-called form of wit, which ridicules by saying the opposite to what you mean.
Peevishness	Includes such whining remarks as: 'You ought to know better.'
Anger	The roar of anger, even if it is under your breath, usually provokes an answering roar.
Suspicion	Often takes the form of being suspicious or even cynical about motives.
Insult	Intentional insults are rare but unintentional ones are not uncommon – especially in replies to applications for jobs.
Accusation	It is obviously difficult to point an accusing finger and maintain courtesy.
Talking down	'In an establishment as large as ours, Miss Smith ...' The didactic or instructional tone grates in letters, and any teaching has to be done with a light touch.
Presumptuousness	Don't presume that someone will do something before they have made up their mind to do it and include this presumption in a letter as it could offend. The line between confidence and presumption is a fine one.

But what are good manners, as opposed to formal politeness? Courtesy results from a mixture of *cordiality* and *tact*: cordiality being the warmth and friendliness you show towards your reader; tact the sensitivity and discretion with which you choose your words.

CASE STUDY: LINCOLN'S LETTERS TO HOOKER AND GRANT

One of the harder tasks of communication is to express confidence to a person while at the same time rejecting some of his words, actions or policies. Former US President Abraham Lincoln, a master of direct, simple communication, demonstrated his ability to face and overcome this problem in his letter to 'Fighting Joe' Hooker – more formally known as Major General Joseph Hooker of the Union Army during the American Civil War.

Lincoln had considerable difficulty in finding a general up to the standard necessary to beat such Confederate Army leaders as Robert E. Lee and 'Stonewall' Jackson. By 1863, General Winfield Scott, the first overall commander of the Union Army and Generals McClellan and Burnside in the eastern theatre of operations had all retired or been discarded by the President.

Despite his careless conversation and insubordinate mien, Hooker had commended himself to Lincoln on account of his offensive spirit. As 1863 unfolded, it became apparent that Hooker was not the man that Lincoln was looking for but his letter is an eloquent testimony to the President's firm attempt to make the most of Hooker's strengths and to minimize his weaknesses by revealing his knowledge of them and a willingness to discount them for the sake of the common cause. His letter reads:

Executive Mansion
Washington
January 26, 1863

To: Major General Hooker

General

I have placed you at the head of the Army of the
Potomac. Of course, I have done this upon what appear to
me to be sufficient reasons. And yet I think it best for you
to know that there are some things in regard to which, I
am not quite satisfied with you. I also believe you do not
mix politics with your profession, in which you are right.
You have confidence in yourself, which is a valuable, if not
an indispensable quality. You are ambitious, which, within
reasonable bounds, does good rather than harm. But I think
that during General Burnside's command of the Army, you
have taken counsel of your ambition, and thwarted him as
much as you could, in which you did a great wrong to the
country, and to a most meritorious and honourable brother
officer. I have heard, in such a way as to believe it, of your
recently saying that both the Army and the Government
needed a Dictator. Of course, it was not *for* this, but in spite
of it, that I have given you the command. Only those
generals who gain successes, can set up dictators. What I now
ask of you is military success, and I will risk the dictatorship.
The government will support you to the utmost of its ability,
which is neither more or less than it has done and will do for
all commanders. I much fear that the spirit which you have
aided to infuse into the Army, of criticizing their
Commander, and withholding confidence from him, will now
turn upon you. I shall assist you as far as I can, to put it
down. Neither you, nor Napoleon, if he were alive again,
could get any good out of an army, while such a spirit
prevails in it.

And now, beware of rashness. Beware of rashness, but

with energy, and sleepless vigilance, go forward, and give us victories.

Yours very truly,
A. Lincoln

By 1864 Lincoln had found his man in General Ulysses Grant. Again the President showed his consummate skill as a communicator, expressing the right balance of discretion, encouragement and caution without in any way detracting from the full delegation of executive action. Like its predecessor, this letter illustrates the principles of simplicity and clarity.

Executive Mansion,
Washington,
April 30, 1864

To: Lieutenant General Grant

Not expecting to see you again before the Spring campaign opens, I wish to express, in this way, my entire satisfaction with what you have done up to this time, so far as I understand it. The particulars of your plans I neither know or seek to know. You are vigilant and self-reliant; and, pleased with this, I wish not to obtrude any constraints or restraints upon you. While I am very anxious that any great disaster, or capture of our men in great numbers, shall be avoided, I know these points are less likely to escape your attention than they would be mine. If there is anything wanting which is within my power to give, do not fail to let me know it.

And now with a brave army, and a just cause, may God sustain you.

Yours very truly,
A. Lincoln

WRITING EFFECTIVE REPORTS

From letters, we move on to reports. The first step is to establish whether a report must stand alone or serve in a supporting role to oral communication of some kind such as a talk, lecture or a briefing. The latter might take the form of the presentation of a draft report to a small committee, followed by another meeting some time later, when the outline and modifications are explained. The report then acts more as an aide-memoire. If the situation allows it, a combination of oral communication and report is preferable, especially if some action is envisaged as a key result.

Your report should begin with an introduction, which sets out the essential background and crystallizes the aim and objectives of the report. The latter will have been already foreshadowed by the title. The format, like a book in miniature, should include the name of the author and the date of compilation. The middle body of evidence, information, issues and discussions should be clearly and succinctly arranged in a simple order, signposted by chapters, major and minor side headings and numbered paragraphs. The concluding section must leave the reader in no doubt as to the writer's conclusions and recommendations.

Your key assumptions should be made manifest at the appropriate places; difficult or technical terms should always be defined. Illustrations, sharing the characteristics of a speaker's good visual aids, can save time and space in the main text, but complicated supporting data should appear as appendices at the end. The minimum requirements for style are not different from those needed for letters or any other forms of business writing. Above all, the report should achieve its stated objective with economy of words, especially where the written word is to be used in alliance with speech.

Brevity

To do our work we all have to read a mass of papers. Nearly all of them are far too long. This wastes time, while energy has to be spent in looking for essential points.

I ask my colleagues and their staff to see that their reports are shorter.

1. The aim should be reports which set out the main points in a series of short, crisp paragraphs.
2. If a report relies on detailed analysis of some complicated factors or on statistics, these should be set out in an appendix.
3. Often the occasion is best met by submitting not a full report, but a reminder consisting of headings only, which can be expounded orally if needed.
4. Let us have an end to such phrases as these: 'it is also important to bear in mind the following considerations ... or consideration should be given to the possibility of carrying into effect ...' Most of these woolly phrases are mere padding, which can be left out altogether, or replaced by a single word. Let us not shrink from using the short expressive phrase, even if it is conversational.

Reports drawn up on the lines I propose may at first seem rough as compared with the flat surface of officialese jargon, but the saving in time will be great, while the discipline of setting out the real points concisely will prove an aid to clearer thinking.

Winston Churchill, former UK Prime Minister, 9 August 1940

Winston Churchill may have enjoyed an unfair advantage over his civil servants in that he had worked for many years as an author and journalist. Both as a writer and orator he had indeed immersed himself exuberantly in the English language as in a tin bath. But the clarity and felicity of his letters and memoranda published later in his six-volume epic *The Second World War* (1948–54) are testomony to a long struggle with the resistances of language to thought, just as the famous Churchillian voice bore the marks of a victory over a childhood speech slur.

For the manager who has grasped the need to be aware of the whole Communication Star and the Five Principles of Good Communication the writing of a report should present few difficulties. Of course Churchill's demand for brevity makes for harder work and greater skill. The long-winded and complicated report takes far less effort. Easy reading makes hard writing.

Moreover false marketing doctrine may persuade us that a thick sheaf of paper, pompous prose and unintelligible diagrams may somehow advertise the importance of the subject and the weight of the conclusions. In fact Albert Sloan's report on General Motors as the company's President and Chairman – perhaps the most influential management report ever written – was not a lengthy or superficially impressive document. The effectiveness of his report lay in the accurate location of the issues raised by organizational size and the practical solutions he proposed. With economy of words the report conveyed the clear thought of the writer and he had ample opportunity to expand it in discussion. Such are the hallmarks of a good report.

The requirements and conventions of the written language are indeed different from the spoken one. But you should endeavour to talk to your reader as if he or she is in the same room in which you are writing. Try reading aloud anything you write and see if it sounds like you. Remember that you are not interested (in this context anyway) in writing literary English, nor have you an academic audience in mind. You are writing in order to be understood and it is you who is writing – no one else. 'Use what language you will,' wrote Ralph Waldo Emerson, the American essayist, poet and philosopher, 'you can never say anything but what you are.'

CHECKLIST:
WILL YOUR REPORT BE EFFECTIVE?

	Yes	No
STRUCTURE AND LAYOUT		
Is the title page complete and well laid out?	☐	☐
Is the layout clear and easy to follow?	☐	☐
Are any essential parts of the structure missing?	☐	☐
Are the main parts of the structure in the most suitable order for this report?	☐	☐
Do headings stand out?	☐	☐
Is the numbering of paragraphs uniform?	☐	☐
Are the appendices clear and helpful?	☐	☐
CONTENT		
Is the summary of abstract (if included) confined to essentials and a fair statement?	☐	☐

Does the Introduction state clearly:	Tick box
The subject and the purpose of the report?	☐
The date of the investigation?	☐
By whom the report was written?	☐
For whom the report was written?	☐
The scope of the report?	☐

	Yes	No
Does the main part of the report contain all the necessary facts and no unnecessary information?	☐	☐
Is the order of the main part of the report right?	☐	☐
Is the problem clearly stated?	☐	☐

Does detail obscure the main issue? ☐ ☐

Are the sources of facts clear? ☐ ☐

Do conclusions follow logically from the facts and their interpretation? ☐ ☐

Are possible solutions abandoned without reason? ☐ ☐

Are terms used, abbreviations and symbols suitable and consistent? ☐ ☐

Are there any statements whose meaning is not quite clear? ☐ ☐

Are facts, figures and calculations accurate? ☐ ☐

GENERAL

Is the report objective? ☐ ☐

Are there criticisms which can be made of the report's recommendation? ☐ ☐

Is the report efficient and businesslike and likely to create a good impression? ☐ ☐

Could a non-technical person directly or indirectly concerned with the report understand it? ☐ ☐

Could anyone reasonably take offence at anything in the report? ☐ ☐

Is the report positive and constructive? ☐ ☐

Does it make clear what decision, if any, is required and by whom? ☐ ☐

KEY POINTS: CLEAR WRITING

- Clear writing begins in the mind. As Goethe wrote: 'If any man wishes to write in a clear style, let him first be clear in his thoughts.'
- There are three elements of writing: structure and layout; content; and style.
- These elements can be artificially analysed and dissected

but they should work together as a whole. Structure and layout can be easily learnt. The critical factor in content is the truth of what you say, for truth is the best communicator. But improving your style does take some thought and effort.

- It's helpful to think of writing – letters, memoranda, reports and emails – as talking to someone on paper. Then you can apply to writing those key Principles of Good Communication – Be Clear, Be Prepared, Be Simple, Be Vivid and Be Natural.

- As with all communication, letter, email and report writing improves in direct ratio to the amount of planning involved. List the major points you want to make in order of importance. Produce a first draft and then 'play' with it until it comes right.

- When speaking, your tone of voice can determine the meaning or import of what you say. Tone is equally present in writing, though harder to get right. It is the musical pitch or vibration in your words that reflects your inner mood or feeling. Make sure – by reading aloud if necessary – that the words in your letter fit the music of your mind.

- Brevity or conciseness is especially important in business or purposeful writing. 'I think,' is much better than, 'In my opinion it is considered not an unjustifiable assumption that'. George Bernard Shaw made the definitive comment here when he handed a letter to a friend by saying: 'I am sorry this letter is so long but I didn't have time to make it short.'

- If this chapter makes it sound easy, remember that writing clearly, simply and understandably is a demanding skill. It takes a lot of hard work to master the art of communicating using the written word – isn't it worth the effort? It's also quite fun.

People think that I can teach them style. What stuff it all is. Have something to say and say it as clearly as you can. That is the only secret of style.

Matthew Arnold, English poet and cultural critic.

7

READING TO SOME PURPOSE

'Reading maketh a full man; conference a
readye man; and writing an exacte man.'
Francis Bacon, English philosopher and writer

''Tis the good reader that makes the good book,' said the
American writer Ralph Waldo Emerson. But what makes a
good reader? Reading is the fourth of the core skills of
communication. Perhaps more than listening it is the forgotten or neglected one. Few books on communication give it
the space it deserves.

One difficulty is that the English language doesn't have
separate terms equivalent to *hearing* and *listening* for the
written or printed word, and so *reading* covers them both.
Reading can be just taking in or comprehending what is on
paper or screen. But good reading is listening in action again,
giving time and thoughtful attention to what you are reading
and remaining alive to all the possibilities it suggests.

Talking books

These are not books, lumps of lifeless paper, but *minds* alive
on the shelves. From each of them goes out its own voice . . .

and just as a touch of the button on our set will fill the room with music, so by taking down one of these volumes and opening it, one can call into range the voice of a man far distant in time and space and hear him speaking to us, mind to mind, heart to heart.

Gilbert Highet, Scottish classicist and US humanities teacher

---

The problems facing the reader who wants a 'good digestible meal' are largely created by the 'poor culinary skills' of the writer. They include:

- Poor structure
- Unattractive appearance and layout
- Turgid and repetitive style
- Unnecessary length
- Lack of examples or illustrations
- Obscure diagrams
- Dense or opaque thought processes
- Too much information
- Too little information
- Unpalatable tone

A good reader, in parallel with a good listener, will not be totally fazed by this surface phenomena, especially if he or she feels that gold lies beneath it. Like a gold prospector and digger you may come away with some gold dust or even a nugget, even though the latter may, on later examination, turn out to be fool's gold.

WHAT IS YOUR READING REQUIREMENT?

Before we go any further it is worth asking yourself about the role or part that reading plays in your professional life. For the moment I am setting aside your reading for pleasure or entertainment, not least because you wouldn't be struggling there with the obstacles I have listed above. The novelists or writers of the books you buy or borrow for fun know how to turn you from a hearer into a listener, so that you cannot wait to turn the page and find out what happens next. That is their craft.

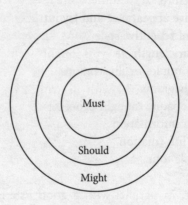

Reading priorities

To help you to clarify your reading requirement go to the core of your job – what are you paid to do? What MUST you read? What SHOULD you read? What MIGHT you read? A consultant neurologist, for example, *must* read certain journals in order to keep up-to-date. He or she *should* read about developments in related fields, such as the care of longterm patients with spinal injuries. The *might* category covers a wide range of possibilities but in this instance it could include reading a book on developments in healthcare in Europe or the US.

Your list will, no doubt, be somewhat similar. Each day on your desk there will be letters, proposals, reports and memos that you *must* read, along with material that falls into the *should* and *might* categories.

Now look again at your job. You are paid, arguably, both to do your job and to improve your job. Does your reading requirement reflect that second dimension? If I may point the question, what have you read in the last six months that has led you to *improve* your existing job as opposed to doing what you were hired to do?

There is also a third dimension. Put briefly, no organization is going to guarantee you the same job for life. We are all on short-term contracts of one kind or another. As well as fulfilling today's role you ought to be preparing for tomorrow's job, one that you may be able only dimly to discern. In other words, with or without the help of your organization or employer, you need to be developing your capability as well as your competence. And reading books, as stores of information and ideas, is a busy element in that process of education or self-development.

If you follow that argument and magnify your reading requirement accordingly, you now face two related problems: *not enough time* and *too much to read*. They seem intractable, because you have all the time there is and no one can give you more of it. Nor can anyone stem the spate of publications. There are, however, two possible solutions: learn to read faster and/or become a more selective reader. Each of these merits further exploration.

SPEED READING

Reading is a skill that we learn slowly and with some difficulty. Some people are slowed down even further by a particular brain difficulty, now called dyslexia. Essentially dyslexia is a disorder in processing patterns of written or printed words. It is the reading equivalent of deafness or colour blindness. With skilful teaching and determination, these people, who are often very intelligent, can make progress and also learn to cope with their disability. But it can be a real handicap.

A child starts to read slowly and aloud because he or she has to make decisions consciously about each word. Children begin to speed up when word recognition develops. Pronouncing the word aloud, so that they can distinguish it by the sound, becomes less necessary.

The ability to read silently is the natural climax to the skill of reading, and indeed it is a comparatively recent one. In ancient times it was the practice for the literate few to read aloud and they were probably unable to read at all without at least audibly mouthing the words. In the fifth century St Augustine of Hippo, while still a young university professor of rhetoric, recorded his admiration for St Ambrose, Bishop of Milan, who he noted – among other things – could read without moving his lips: 'His eye glided over the pages . . . but his voice and tongue were at rest.'

One frequent symptom of a below-average-speed reader is the persistence into adulthood of lip movements or any physical throat tremors, like those of a ventriloquist. One test is to place a finger on your Adam's apple and see if it moves while you are reading silently. For those who still mouth words, a course in reading techniques may prove invaluable.

Studies show that the average speed an educated person in the West can read without losing full comprehension of the meaning is about 200–250 words per minute, provided the subject matter is reasonably easy – a short novel, for example. This speed is attained by an averagely intelligent child by about the age of thirteen years; a university graduate will probably average between 300 and 500 words a minute, with some exceptional readers close to 1,000 words.

Some of the techniques evolved at Harvard University several decades ago for doubling reading speed include: flashing screens produced by an awesome-sounding machine called a tachistoscope; blinds that move down the lines of a page; films of print moving at different speeds; and carefully graded exercises These battery-hen methods made it all look too scientific. The theory was that our eyes move in five or six jerks along a line, pausing while we read in 'fixation'. According to the 'school of speed reading' the secret is to train the eyes to take in each line in only one or two jerks. The variety of exercises and visual aids mentioned above are designed to induce the reader to adopt this habit.

Personally I do not find this advice very helpful. Once I start getting self-conscious about my eye movements I forget what I am reading about. My suggestion would be to relax the eye muscles, forget about eye jerks and let the eyes move smoothly and evenly along the line of words, like a scythe regularly sweeping down the long grass.

It is easy to test your speed by roping off a piece of prose and reading it against the clock. But you have to test yourself for comprehension as well. If the material is average in diffi-culty – an article in a 'quality' newspaper, for example – you should be able to read it at not less than about 300 words a minute. The British writer Arnold Bennett estimated the average book reviewer's speed at eight words per second, which gives 480 words a minute. An Irish professor, doubtless training on Irish whiskey, has claimed 4,200 words per minute. If you are much slower, a full reading course, tachistoscope and all, is recommended. Or you may like to try one of the Do-It-Yourself manuals on the subject. But if it is a question of tuning up the engine, all that is needed is some practice. Once our reading habits are set it is hard to change them. And we owe a great deal to those who taught us to read silently, swiftly and with understanding when we were young.

'I am not a speed reader,' said the US science fiction writer Isaac Asimov, 'I am a speed understander.' Mere physical speed in reading isn't going to help you very much. For at a certain point on the speedometer you will lose understanding and then comprehension.

In a nutshell

I took a course in speed reading, learning to read straight down the middle of the page, and was able to read War and Peace *in twenty minutes. It's about Russia.*

Woody Allen, US film director and actor

Not that there is any special merit in reading slowly, as if that somehow confers more understanding. As the French mathematician and philosopher Blaise Pascal wrote: 'When we read too fast or too slowly, we understand nothing.'

SELECTIVE READING

A second defensive strategy against the growing amount of paperwork is simply to read less of it. In practice that often means sticking to a MUST circle and forgetting about the

SHOULD and MIGHT rings of reading requirement. Is there a better way?

Let me review the story in outline. Take a Bible and look at its contents, for example. A 'Bible', from the Greek word *biblos*, literally meaning 'book', is in fact the original library of the ancient Jews. You can see that it contains their whole literature: written-down stories, instruction manuals, chronicles or histories, proverbs and collections of prophecies, all under one cover. The Greeks and even the Romans could have compiled similar libraries of their key books – beginning with the works of the Greek poet Homer – in what we would regard as two or three fat volumes. The fifteenth-century classical scholar and humanist Erasmus and his generation were the last to be able to read all the books of any significance – the sum of human knowledge – in existence for them at the time (this did not, of course, include the literatures of China, India or Arabia for reasons of discovery and language).

The invention of the printing press brought these libraries – the Bible and the classics – to much wider audiences than the wealthy or learned few who possessed handwritten books. By dint of translating them into vernacular languages, the printers reached even more readers and created a market for yet more books in English, both sacred and secular. The trickle of books and papers became a 'Victoria Falls' of publication. Now no library in the world has space or money to contain, let alone keep up with, this immense flood of paper, although some – like the US Library of Congress and the British Library – make a valiant effort to do so. Even if such a library existed, your life is too short to do more than nibble at this profusive offering. Putting it all on to computers won't help – you still have to read it.

Not only books but every form of publication has multiplied in response to market forces. Take newspapers. On my shelves I have a copy of one of the earliest newspapers in England, the *Mercurius Aulicus*. The Royalists printed it in Oxford during the English Civil War. One weekly edition covering all national events is about five A5-sized pages. Compare that to your Sunday newspaper for size! People presumably want quantity and bulk, at a low price, and that is what newspaper proprietors provide. It's odd when you reflect that radio and television have arguably made the news function of the press almost totally redundant.

One possibility is to let others select what you read, always assuming that you have a staff. Very busy people, such as chief executives of companies or heads of government departments, do rely upon trained staffs in this way. The danger, of course, is that they select reading material for you on the wrong criteria, so that you don't get to read what is in your MUST and SHOULD circles of requirement. But this problem is soluble by good communication based on mutual trust, assuming you have both selected and trained your staff carefully to know your mind.

Even the majority of us who do not have staff working for and under us can be helped by others to select what we read. Some people rely more on word of mouth than others when it comes to choosing which novels to read. Personally I operate much the same principle over books on management or leadership, which obviously fall somewhere in my own 'Three Circles' of reading requirement. If I hear two or three people mentioning a particular book – especially if I respect their judgement – it goes on my list. The selection and advice of specialists – the function of the book reviewer – can also save us much time.

THE SKILL OF SCANNING

So much for the strategy. By some self-managed or delegated process – or perhaps a combination of the two – the piece of writing has now arrived on your desk, be it actual or virtual. As I have said, the written paper may be anything from an email or letter to a journal or book. Your next tactical step is to *scan* the material in order to judge how much time and attention it needs or merits.

Our word 'skill' probably comes from one or two Old Norse words meaning respectively 'to distinguish' or 'to decide'. The habitual 'decisions' or skill of coordinating eye movements with meaning is one aspect of reading. The other skill lies in making accurate judgements in what to read, at what level of thoroughness. For, as the British philosopher Francis Bacon reminds us, 'Some books are to be read only in parts; others to be read, but not curiously; and some few to be read wholly, and with diligence and attention.' The skill of changing gear, and adjusting speed to the material, we might call the skill of *scanning*.

Scanning involves the action of quickly glancing down the body of text so that the mind can rapidly take in the gist of what is written. The word 'scan' comes from the Latin *scandere* meaning 'to climb or leap', so imagine yourself as jumping quickly from stepping stone to stepping stone without getting your feet wet in the text. It should be a wide, sweeping, methodical search, quick but not hasty. *Festine lente*, 'make haste slowly'. Scanning should also be an intensive examination, not a superficial one. It takes time, but it will save you time.

This moving survey from point to point gives you an overall picture. It may lead you to scrutinize parts of the written piece. 'Scrutiny' is another word we took from Latin;

it derives from the word *scrutinium* meaning 'trash or rubbish'. So the original scrutiny took place on the rubbish dumps of ancient Rome as the poor sorted out usable rags. It stresses close attention to minute detail. Your thoughtful attention – the essence of good reading as of good listening – has now moved from wide angle to narrow focus:

- Prepare by previewing the *content* of the piece that interests you – study the title, sub-headings, illustrations, and writer's aims in writing.
- Look at the writer's pattern – the structure plan or *method* that he or she has adopted – the table of contents, rough lengths of chapters, appendices and notes.
- Sample one or two paragraphs to test the writing – density of thought, tone, intelligibility, the 'ring of truth'.
- Scan – if still interested – the whole or selected parts, looking more closely for the necklace thread of the argument or theme – key paragraphs, sentences or words.
- Develop actual reading speed with long rhythmic eye sweeps, both horizontal and vertical.
- Examine more closely the parts or passages that especially interest you, rereading where necessary.

In order to do this more effectively you may have to rid yourself of two rules that tend to be indoctrinated in us from infancy. They are:

- Always start at the beginning and read through to the end.
- Always move your eyes from left to right – or right to left for some languages – horizontally over the page.

Both are good rules for those first learning to read but they inhibit the person who wants to develop the advanced skill of scanning.

The main danger of scanning is that speed can lead to a gradual loss of control. Like the listener, the reader's first duty is to grasp what the other person means. Depending on the ability of the writer, this can be an easy or near-impossible task. One has to stop and check frequently. Is that what he or she means? What are they really getting at? If one scans too fast it is easy to misjudge a corner and end up in the ditch of culpable ignorance. 'But you *should* have read my letter more carefully . . .' may be the epitaph on your promotion prospects.

We are sometimes inhibited from free perusal or scanning by the second rule: the ingrained sense that *proper* reading means the jerking of the eyes so many times to the right at each line of print. Having freed ourselves from an unthinking adherence to this rule we can develop long rhythmic eye sweeps, zipping vertically down the middle of a page. Additionally we may opt for still less time and employ what the French called *coup d'œil*, the rapid glance that takes in a whole page at a time. Margins help this movement because they act like picture frames. Indeed, it is possible to imagine each page or section as a picture. Individual words are like bricks: it is the message on the wall that matters.

Lastly, you do have to mean business when you are reading. Take a positive but not reverential attitude to the report, article or book in hand. It reminds me of some days when I worked as a deep-sea fisherman. Like a deckhand on an Arctic trawler gutting fish, you have no time to be squeamish. Your 'knife' must go in and 'slit' the book or report down the middle, laying bare that one sentence or paragraph that is the still-beating heart of the written piece. The idea of swiftly and skilfully 'gutting' a book or report may seem repellent but that is the reality of reading in a world where books, reports or articles fall on our decks in massive shoals.

So we have to rid ourselves once and for all of the idea that the reader has a moral duty to read every word when he or she takes up a written piece. 'What, have you not read it through?' the Scottish author James Boswell once asked. 'No, Sir,' replied his friend Dr Johnson, 'do *you* read books *through*?'

CHECKLIST:
READING CAREFULLY

	Yes	No
Are you clear about your purpose in reading any piece of writing with this depth of interest and attention?	☐	☐
Have you some definite questions in mind that you are seeking to answer?	☐	☐
Are they the right questions?	☐	☐
Do you constantly ask yourself questions as you read to stay focused on the subject?	☐	☐
Do you read for main ideas? Can you identify the main idea in each chapter, and the contributing ideas in each section and each paragraph?	☐	☐
Do you critically test the evidence, explanations, examples and other detail offered as grounds for the writer's case?	☐	☐
Have you suitable methods of making notes or recording what you learn or can use?	☐	☐
Do you match or compare the writer's experience with your own? If so, does your experience lend weight to the writer's conclusions?	☐	☐
Is any of it worth reading again (now or later on)?	☐	☐
Should you discuss the material with anyone? (Who? Why? When? How? What?)	☐	☐

KEY POINTS: READING TO SOME PURPOSE

- 'What is reading but silent conversation?' asked the English writer and poet Walter Savage Landor. The art of reading is akin to the art of listening. Both involve hearing or reading with thoughtful attention, together with a certain economy or grace of effort.

- Writers, like speakers, can pose numerous unintended problems to the reader. A poor or unskilled reader will be thrown by these obstacles, possibly missing the pearl of meaning that lies somewhere within. A good reader, by contrast, overcomes these difficulties.

- What is your requirement? Apart from the priorities – MUST, SHOULD and MIGHT – of your present job and the need to improve the job, add the requirement to develop your potential for tomorrow's tasks. Books and written material play an important part in preparing yourself. What five books, apart from this one, do you plan to work upon in the next twelve months? Remember the US author Mark Twain's words: 'The person who does not read good books has no advantage over the man who can't read them.'

- The explosion of the printed word poses problems. You need to read a lot, your time is limited, and – to make matters worse – there is an ever-growing mountain of information available. There are two possible solutions: to read faster and to select rigorously.

- Speed-reading may help, especially if you are naturally a slow reader. But it will not cut down the time bill dramatically. For thoughtful attention and haste cannot sleep in the same bed.

- The principal answer is to be very selective in what you choose to read (beyond the MUST area where you have no choice). Always go for quality rather than quantity. Get the recommendations or professional advice.

- Whatever comes your way by necessity or choice, scan it well first in order to determine at what level you will be reading. Then make the appropriate response, which may be the waste-paper basket or further examination and scrutiny perhaps over several readings, until you have extracted all the juices you need.
- To read without reflecting is like eating without digestion.

Reading is to the mind what exercise is to the body.
English proverb

PART THREE

COMMUNICATION AT WORK

8

PRACTICAL PRESENTATION SKILLS

As I mentioned earlier, my first encounter with presentations was in the army. The military had developed the method out of research into types of instruction carried out during the Second World War. A presentation, as I have defined already, is a formal or set-piece occasion with two usual hallmarks:

- The use of audio-visual aids
- Teamwork

With regard to the latter characteristic, you can give a presentation of your own but it is more usual to use the names of *talk*, *lecture*, *address* or *seminar* for such solo efforts.

Not only did presentations play a part in teaching me to become an officer but later, when I was a civilian senior lecturer in military history at Sandhurst for seven years, one of my responsibilities was to teach the art of presentation to the officer cadets. As part of their obligatory military history course (now renamed war studies) the cadets had to lead or take part in presentations held in the theatre-like college model rooms to their intakes on famous battles or campaigns, such as the D-Day landings. Veterans of these engagements often commented afterwards. My job included giving some further lessons on the battle and then a constructive critique of the presentation skills. The department, I may add, also had to do some presentations as well.

Since those days the practice has now spread into industry and commerce, so that *presentation* has almost taken over from *public speaking* as a general term. Plenty of occasions arise, such as:

- Making a marketing or sales proposal
- Launching a new product or service
- Speaking at a seminar or conference
- Running a training session
- Presenting your business plan

Please add two other examples from your own field. Try to think ahead. If your career plans work out, what sort of occasions for speaking in public will arise?

You can see at once the importance of presentational skills for you. Quite apart from the impact they may have on your business in terms of bottom-line results, presentations are also high-profile events for you personally. To some extent you will be on trial and you will be judged. In some contexts your career or progress may even depend upon your performances.

Therefore your aim should be to develop your presentational skills, based on the Communication Star framework in Chapter 2 (page 20), so that you can present with confidence and effect upon all the occasions that are likely to arise. The actor going on stage is confident that he or she knows the lines and has the professional skills and experience to seize and hold the attention of an audience. Notice, however, the importance here of *context* – the theatre in general and this particular play or production.

As with all analogies, the comparison between you and an actor will break down at a certain point. You will almost certainly not be mouthing someone else's lines, nor will you be wearing greasepaint or a period costume. More importantly, you are directing and producing your own performance, as well as writing the script and delivery on stage. But the analogy is a strong one, for it suggests to me six main clusters of presentational skill:

- PROFILING THE OCCASION, AUDIENCE AND LOCATION
- PLANNING AND WRITING THE PRESENTATION
- USING VISUAL AIDS
- PREPARING YOUR TALK
- REHEARSING WITH OTHERS
- DELIVERING ON THE DAY

All of these are important, for each contributes to your overall effectiveness as a presenter. You may not be able to control or manage some of the factors – locations, for example – but you should ensure that everything that can be done to ensure success has been done. You will then approach the day with your natural apprehension balanced by a growing confidence and expectation of success.

PROFILING THE OCCASION, AUDIENCE AND LOCATION

When it comes to presentations the first thing you need is to be clear what business you are in, and conversely, what business you are not in. For example, more often than not I turn down requests for after-dinner speeches because I am not in the entertainment business. Nor do I usually accept invitations to speak at sales conferences, for I am not a motivational speaker. Unless you are a genius you cannot take every part in the play. Know the limits of your business and within it know the limits of your own professional abilities.

Granted that this particular occasion – actual or envisaged – falls squarely within your proper sphere, it follows that you will probably have had some sort of experience of similar occasions. Therefore you will have a rough idea of the audience and you may even have used that particular location before. But as a professional you need to check out all three: *occasion*, *audience* and *location*. Consider the case study below:

> The Nympho Airline was short of cash and hired pilots that other airlines had long since rejected or discarded such as Captain Nimrod. On his first day Nimrod sat down in the cockpit of Nympho's only jumbo jet and balanced his brandy flask on the autopilot unit. 'Let's get going,' he said to the crew. 'I know all about these jumbo jets. I am an experienced pilot. We are going to Tunisia, aren't we? Been there many times. No, don't confuse me with the route plan or weather forecast – we always get there in the end. Just turn left at Marseilles. Come on, don't waste time checking fuel levels – the ground engineers will have done that. Switch on engines. What is the dinner menu tonight?'

To ensure that you avoid the disasters awaiting the Captain Nimrods of this world and their kind, I suggest that you work through the checklist below. Its purpose is to bring the event into sharper focus, so that you can shape the most appropriate presentation for it. I have divided the checklist into three sections, but you should always remember to think holistically about presentations. Occasion, audience and location are interactive. I have known one otherwise successful conference virtually ruined by the slowness of service and very low quality of food in the hotel (not booked by me I might add!).

CHECKLIST:
PROFILING THE OCCASION, AUDIENCE AND LOCATION

	Yes	No
THE OCCASION		
Do you know the aim or objective of the presentation?	☐	☐
Are you clear what kind of occasion it is?	☐	☐
Is there sufficient time for the presentation?	☐	☐
Has time been allowed for discussion?	☐	☐
Do you know who will chair the session and introduce you?	☐	☐
Do they have biographical information about you?	☐	☐
Have you grasped the context – what is happening before and after – of your presentation?	☐	☐
THE AUDIENCE		
Do you know its size?	☐	☐
Can you assess their motivation for being there?	☐	☐
Have you an accurate idea of their expectations?	☐	☐
Is the knowledge level of the audience in relation to your subject:		
High?	☐	☐
Mixed?	☐	☐
Low?	☐	☐

Do you know any of them personally or professionally? ☐ ☐

All in all, do you expect them to be:

Unusually friendly? ☐ ☐

Indifferent? ☐ ☐

Hostile? ☐ ☐

Will they be able to use what they hear? ☐ ☐

THE LOCATION

Have you a clear picture in your mind of the following:

Room size? ☐ ☐

Seating arrangements? ☐ ☐

Platform/lectern? ☐ ☐

Acoustics? ☐ ☐

Public address equipment? ☐ ☐

Audio-visual equipment? ☐ ☐

Technical assistance? ☐ ☐

Room temperature? ☐ ☐

Lighting controls? ☐ ☐

Refreshments? ☐ ☐

You can sometimes meet your audience in advance if your presentation is part of a series, as at a conference. You can then sense the audience and how they react. It's helpful to think of an audience as not merely a collection of individuals – although it is that – but as a whole that is more than the sum of its parts, or, in other words, as a social entity that has a life and personality of its own.

That assumes, of course, that the audience has been together for some time. If so, you will obviously have an advantage if you can see them in action responding to another speaker or presentation. At least you may learn what not to do! If the audience is assembling just to hear you and your colleagues, remember that they may not know each other (even if they work in the same organization). You will then need to show awareness that they, like yourself, are in a new and perhaps unfamiliar situation. If time and the size of the group allow, it may make sense to encourage the participants to introduce themselves briefly and to outline their expectations.

Locations should always be visited, if possible well before the event. It is all too easy to make *false assumptions about places*. What is a large room to some people is a small one to others. Recently I was invited to conduct a seminar in the presidential suite of an international hotel in an African country. I imagined a palatial set of rooms. In fact I found the twelve participants huddled around the presidential dining table in a room that lacked space for an overhead projector and screen. Always remember the venerable military maxim: 'Time spent on reconnaissance is seldom wasted.' Go and look.

PLANNING AND WRITING THE PRESENTATION

At this point you will need a pen and paper and/or your personal computer. You are now clear about what the occasion is, what is expected of you, who the audience will be and how large it is, and what the location looks like. And, after your negotiations with the organizers, you will also have the limits of the time frame you will share with the audience – the length of time available and at your disposal. Now the real work starts.

What is your objective?

It's good practice to state your objective or objectives at the beginning of your presentation and why you think it or they are important. Therefore you need to be clear in your own mind about what you are *aiming* to do and why it is worthwhile.

In this context it's useful to make a distinction between general and specific purpose. Purpose in the general sense can be qualified but not defined. Your general purpose may, for example, be educational, religious, political or commercial. It will be implicit if not explicit in the business you are in. Indeed, it is that general purpose which determines the nature of your business and it will almost certainly underline your presentation.

Your purpose or objective for the presentation, however, needs to be much more sharply focused. It should have at least some of the following key characteristics of a well-set objective. Tick the box if you have a particular presentation in mind and your objective meets these criteria.

Clear	☐	Realistic	☐
Specific	☐	Challenging	☐
Measurable	☐	Worthwhile	☐
Time-bounded	☐	Participative	☐

Not all of these criteria will be relevant. You may find it hard to MEASURE your effectiveness in achieving your objective in an educational presentation, for example, as opposed to a commercial pitch to prospective customers. Nor will it always be possible to get the audience to PARTICIPATE in agreeing the objective.

The TIME-BOUNDED criterion is especially important.

Many presentations fail because the presenter attempts to achieve too much in the time available. If you have only twenty minutes to explain a new lawn-mower product to a convention of garden centre buyers you don't have time to sketch in the whole story of humanity's application of machinery to practical problems, together with a discourse on the evolution of the modern garden. You can CHALLENGE yourself and the audience, but only if you are REALISTIC about what can be done in the time available.

Make a plan

Having written down your objective or objectives, focused at the right level of specificity for the occasion, your next job is to sketch out a framework or skeleton of your presentation. Reduced to its most simple form it should have a BEGINNING, MIDDLE and END (see table overleaf).

With planning it's best to take several bites at the cherry. Allow plenty of time for your depth mind or unconscious to work on the problem. For example, I made my first plan for this chapter some months ago, but I have revised it several times since then. For on each occasion I found that I had come to a different conclusion. Of course you do have to draw the line somewhere, bearing in mind that no one ever makes a perfect plan. That is why some books are never finished – only abandoned! You are looking for a workable, feasible plan – not a perfect one.

Before you go into production, why not show your plan to the sponsors of the event if there are any? Several minds are better than one at this stage of planning. Weigh and consider any constructive comments, then make the necessary amendments, even if it means going back to the drawing board.

PLANNING THE PRESENTATION	
PHASE	**NOTES**
Beginning	Introduction by chairman.
	Your introductory remarks.
	State your objective(s) and give some reasons why they are relevant to the audience.
	Signpost the main outlines of the presentation.
Middle	Break the complex whole of the presentation down into manageable parts, just as an author divides a book into chapters. Three, four, five or six sections, usually no more.
	Make sure that you illustrate main points by examples or support them by evidence.
	A half-time summary is often a good idea, especially if it is a longish and complicated presentation.
	Put a time estimate against each of these parts or sections and double check that most time goes on top priorities.
End	A summary is often a good way to initiate the last phase.
	Don't leave your conclusions to chance. Refer back to your objective and prepare your final remarks with that in mind.

USING VISUAL AIDS

'A picture is worth a thousand words', as the Chinese proverb says. Why? Because we take in much of our information – more than 50 per cent – through the gateway of our eyes. Therefore there is always a strong case for using visual aids, especially if your presentation is primarily about conveying information.

Whether or not you make them yourself on your computer or commission others to make them, remember to apply three of the Five Principles of Good Communication – Be Clear, Be Simple and Be Vivid. The art of slideshow making is to know what to leave out. If you are going to give much the same presentation more than once it is highly advisable to get the best professional help available to you in the design and making of your visual aids. If you tell a specialist what you want to communicate, they should be able to help you to encapsulate and support your message on slide or digitally.

Some general tips on using visual aids

- Use a series of pictures to structure your presentation for you and allow you to look at the audience while developing each point. Look at the audience more than the pictures on the screen.
- Present only essential information on each picture.
- Restrict the content to about twenty-five words or the equivalent in figures.
- Make sure any slides or frames are clearly numbered in the correct sequence and are the right way up. Any confusion will damage your professional image.
- Use pictures, drawings and colour for interest – 'A picture is worth a thousand words,' remember.
- Don't leave any one visual aid on for too long.
- Above all, do not overload your presentation with too many slides or pictures – 'Less is more'.
- If you're using hi-tech equipment then make sure you have someone on hand who can help with any technical hitches – this includes everything from locating powerpoints to dealing with stalled slideshows.

If you really are trying to sell a lawnmower at that garden centre convention, why not produce the actual lawnmower, together with a short video of it demolishing the hay in the back garden? Your product is always your best visual aid in such commercial presentations.

Visual aids are important and I have always had a passion for them. For I prefer to look with my audience at a picture, to share and explore it together. It reflects a fundamental concept about communication. My concept or model of communication is actually more A than B in relation to the diagram below:

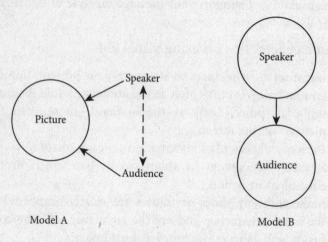

Two models of communication

Model A above reminds me of some words that the French aviator, poet and writer Antoine de Saint-Exupéry wrote many years ago: 'Life has taught us that love is not gazing into each other's eyes but looking together in the same direction.'

PREPARING YOUR TALK

Unless you have a modern and sophisticated autocue system at your disposal, such as prominent politicians use at major conferences, I would counsel against reading from a written script. Doing so certainly has the advantage of greater accuracy, but it loses your eye contact with your audience. An experienced speaker using a written script, like Winston Churchill for example, can glance up frequently and make it sound more natural. But even then the disadvantages outweigh the advantages, especially as we now live in an age that values informality.

When should you read a written presentation? Giving a radio talk is one such occasion, for exact timing matters and you cannot see your audience to make eye contact. Even in the radio studio, however, you will probably find yourself looking up from your script and addressing the invisible audience – actors in radio plays certainly do so.

Perhaps if you have to give a scientific paper or some prestigious lecture that will be published, writing it down and reading it out will be expected of you. Even then it may make more communication sense to give your audience the written paper before or after your presentation and content yourself with presenting it rather than reading it out verbatim. In communication, speaking and writing perform different but related or overlapping functions and it is unwise to confuse them.

At the other end of the spectrum, why not speak without notes? If you are a professional speaker, you should always do so. It is not such a difficult art to master as you may think. Actors, comedians and concert musicians do not refer to notes so why should you? The practice of doing so leaves you free to look at your audience and to think on your feet.

It does take more time in preparation but it is invariably worth it.

By 'learning the part' I don't mean committing a fully written-out script to memory, as the actor or comedian or musician does before going on stage. You have to memorize the plan – the structure or skeleton of your presentation – together with any facts, quotations, stories or examples. The test is that you must be confident that you can give the presentation without recourse to notes. Your short-term memory is probably much more trustworthy than you imagine. Does it matter if you get the odd word or phrase wrong?

In between the extremes of reading out a prepared script and talking without notes there are several other options. If it is a 'one-off' presentation and if you lack confidence to abandon your notes altogether, you could use your computer slides or flipcharts as notes. Or you could prepare prompt cards, with a punch hole in the corner and some string to hold them in order and for ease in turning over. Another possibility is to have your presentation outline on a large sheet of paper in front of you on the lectern, but out of sight of the audience.

Whatever method you choose to employ, you do need to decide upon it in the planning phase and then work hard like an actor to imprint your presentation within your short-term memory. Even actors sometimes have a prompter in the wings should they forget their lines. Keep a copy of your presentation notes on you or near you so that you can glance at it again on stage. Never be afraid to fish it out and look at it during your presentation if you momentarily lose your bearings.

REHEARSING WITH OTHERS

A rehearsal is a private performance or a practice session prior to a public performance. You may need more than one rehearsal before an important presentation. But you can over-rehearse, which kills spontaneity and therefore offends the Communicaton Principle of Be Natural. A good orchestra will rehearse several times but leave something in reserve to come out on the night of the actual performance.

If you are presenting as part of a team it is essential to have a rehearsal or two, preferably in the place where you will give the presentation. The mutual constructive criticism that follows will lead to improvements. This practice session allows you to tune up your own instrument, going through your part and hearing the sound of your own voice in that particular room. It promotes a smooth and graceful co-ordination of effort among the team. Lastly, it enables you to check out all the equipment and visual aids. Are they legible from the back row or far corner of the room, for instance?

Setting the stage

In a theatre, stage management is the organizing or mechanics of effective presentation. It includes setting the stage, lighting it, providing the right properties at the right time and in the right place. The stage manager's job is to manage all these mechanics so that the actor doesn't have to think about them. If anything goes seriously wrong every member of the audience is going to see it and there is no possible way in which the stage manager could explain why it has gone wrong or to justify its going wrong. It had just gone wrong and from that moment it is irretrievable in the minds of the audience. If something happens for which he or she feels the need to apologize, or should apologize, then he or she has failed.

A good stage manager's attitude of mind is therefore at all times one of using his or her imagination to anticipate every conceivable disaster that could or might occur. The stage manager does it by mentally going through every operation that every actor and every member of the stage staff might have to perform, and checks to see that everything has been done to see that the operation can be performed as easily and as safely as possible. It's his or her job to see that nothing happens that will distract actors and audience from their close interaction with each other.

John Casson, 'Are You Getting Through?', *Industrial Society*, November 1970

Even if you are speaking on your own and you decide against actual practice sessions – as opposed to mental rehearsals that really are essential – you should always take the earliest opportunity to reconnoitre the place, checking the seating arrangements, lighting and acoustics, potential external or internal distractions, and any equipment that is being supplied for your use. You should not be satisfied until you (or someone you trust) have seen the equipment in question working. In my experience the things that can go wrong with any form of mechanical equipment, not least computers, are legion. 'I'm sorry, I am not used to this particular model,' hisses the operator apologetically as the machine breaks down.

But it is you as the presenter who carries the responsibility: you will have communicated to your audience that you have failed to observe the Communication Principle of Be Prepared. Remember that your audience may well have read this book as well as you! Of course, you will gain marks if you show unflappability or even fish out the odd spare part from your pocket – but who wants to live dangerously?

DELIVERING ON THE DAY

If you have done your homework you shouldn't encounter any big surprises when you come to give your presentation. There may, however, be some changes 'on the day' that you haven't anticipated and you must make a judgement about making any changes in the content or methods of your presentation. Having done that, you and the audience are ready to go on the journey together. Now all depends on your delivery skills.

SPEAKING SKILLS	
PHASE	**NOTES AND TIPS**
Beginning	If the chairman's introduction needs amendment do it courteously and with thanks.
	Capture your audience. Explain the background and objectives for the presentation in as concise, clear and vital a way as possible, giving your audience time to tune into your voice and accustom themselves to you as a person.
	Tell them what you intend to do.
Middle	'Grace, pace and space' – the hallmarks of a good motor car – should characterize your presentation.
	Keep it moving as you cover with professional ease your prepared points.
	Let the audience know in advance if you want them to ask clarifying questions as you talk or to save them until after you have finished.
	Try to sweep the whole audience with your eyes as you speak, so that everyone feels included.
	Remember to vary the tone of your voice and not to speak too fast or too low.
	Look pleasant – people like looking at someone who appears to be enjoying himself or herself.

End	Signal to your audience when you are entering the ending phase.
	Don't introduce new ideas or information but consolidate what you have done.
	End on a high note if you can: a short, strong conclusion.
	Always prepare carefully and learn your last two or three sentences.
Questions/ Discussion	Repeat any questions that may be inaudible to parts of the audience.
	Try not to be long-winded in answering them.
	Promote discussion by asking a few questions of your own.
	Make sure that all the lights are on in this phase. Be courteous always and express appreciation.
	Disentangle multi-part questions and answer each part separately.
Conclusion	Avoid the session petering out by further summarizing the discussion and reinforcing any action points.
	Close with some words of thanks.

The news that you are going to take part in a presentation is enough to set the alarm bells ringing in most people's minds. No wonder that most people are often plagued by nerves before such public exposures. Perhaps you may be one of them. How can you learn to cope with nerves?

CHECKLIST:
ARE YOU A NERVOUS SPEAKER?

	Yes	No
Do you ever feel self-conscious if you have to stand up and speak to a group, even if you know them quite well?	☐	☐
Do you experience difficulty in finding the right words to express yourself clearly?	☐	☐
Do you get unpleasant symptoms, such as palpitations, feeling sick, a dry mouth, sweaty palms or breathlessness?	☐	☐
Does your mind ever go completely blank before you stand up to speak?	☐	☐
Do you fear it might and that you will then forget what you were going to say and make a fool of yourself?	☐	☐

As you may already have discovered, there are ways of overcoming nerves. The first step is to realize that nerves are normal so don't be alarmed by them. Some degree of nervous tension before a presentation is actually a good thing. It gets the adrenalin flowing and prepares your mind and body for a superlative performance. Some simple relaxation exercises, like deep breathing, can help to keep these pre-event nerves in a manageable state.

Why does it happen? Your body cannot distinguish too well between danger situations. Prompted by your mind, it interprets a public presentation as a danger situation, which arouses anxiety if not fear. Why should it do this? Probably because being watched by a large number of people reminds our primitive selves of being potential victims under observation from hungry predators or enemies lying in wait in an ambush. Our body changes prepare us for fight or flight. If you are wounded in a fight, for example, it's better not to have food in your stomach. So it is natural to feel or be sick on the threshold of perceived danger situations.

You can see that *perception* plays a large part in keeping these natural physical reactions within manageable proportions. No actor could go on stage every night if he or she perceived the audience to be hostile. There are occasionally hostile audiences but on the whole we go to the theatre in a positive frame of mind, wanting to be entertained or enlightened and willing the cast to succeed. Half the battle is to persuade yourself that the audience is on your side, either already or potentially so. Why else would they have come?

When speaking on formal occasions you can move about if you wish. But the most comfortable anchor stance is to have your feet placed slightly apart and the weight of the body thrown slightly forward on to the balls of the feet. There is then no fidgeting or unnecessary movement. Gestures spring spontaneously from the words that are on your lips.

All movement is potentially expressive of personality. Nervous fidgeting can send the wrong signals. You can learn to control it. Constant smoothing of the hair, a rhythmic rising on the toes, fiddling with markers, pens or glasses, swaying from side to side, pacing to and fro, fastening or unfastening of a button, the jangling of coins or keys in a pocket, all these are merely controllable nervous habits. Do anything you like with your hands but don't have them in the same place the whole time.

Lastly, remember that a presentation is theatre. Act as if you are already in possession of supreme self-confidence. Be a little larger than life and let your enthusiasm show on your face. We are all geese pretending to be swans. Even swans, you remember, may seem to sail with lordly indifference, but underneath they are paddling energetically to keep going. Here are some paddles for you:

THE SIX PHYSICAL STEPS TO CONFIDENCE	
KEY AREA	**NOTES**
Breathe deeply	Breathe well down into your lungs. This enables your diaphragm to control the release of breath from your lungs as you utter each word.
Manage your hands	If your hands seem to 'get in your way', clasp them loosely in front of you, or place them behind your back. Train yourself to forget them.
Look at your audience	Look at your audience all the time you are speaking and embrace them all in your glance. Try to forget yourself in the urge to communicate.
Move well	Let your movements be deliberate and *unhurried*. In a big hall, make them a little larger than life.
Talk slowly	Do not let your rate of utterance exceed your rate of thought. Only so can you avoid the danger of 'stumbling' over your words. In fact, do not think of *words* now – think only of ideas and mind pictures.
Compose and relax	Always allow yourself some minutes to clear your mind of the matters that have been occupying it before the presentation. Compose yourself and relax. Your audience will do the same.

A good presentation should be like a performance by a world-class orchestra. When you sit back merely to enjoy – not technically to analyse – a piece of music, are you consciously aware of the 'pom-pom, pom-pom' of the trombones, the trill of the flute and so on, as separate components of the work? Are you not rather aware of the entire symphonic effect of the *combination* of sounds?

If a speech pleases, grips, interests, informs – the qualities essential to a speech – it is not because you are conscious of the effect of each of its components. It is because the whole attitude of the speaker combines to produce an *overall* effectiveness. Knowledge, design, narrative, all the arts of good delivery, are combined to make communication effective. As a contemporary said of the famous Greek orator Demosthenes, 'He that only *hears* Demosthenes loses much the better part of the oration.'

KEY POINTS: PRACTICAL PRESENTATION SKILLS

- Presentations are addresses to an audience using audio-visual aids and usually involving more than one person working together as a team. You need to be able to take an effective part in a presentation and know how to lead such a team. There are six pillars of success.
- PROFILING the occasion, the audience and the location allows you the strength of fore knowledge. To be forewarned is to be forearmed. In this context it is the way to apply the Communication Principle of Be Prepared.
- PLANNING your presentation, with a structure of general points supported by detail, will give you the framework for success.
- SELECTING the right visual aids is a major step towards ensuring that your presentation is going to be effective. Make certain that any visual aids you use are *clear*, *simple* and *vivid*.
- PREPARING your talk embraces both committing what you are going to say to your short-term memory and preparing any prompt notes. You should aim to talk without notes. Seldom if ever should you read from a script.

- REHEARSING is a recipe for success. It builds confidence before the actual performance. Included under this heading is checking out that the 'stage management' aspects of the presentation are all in hand.
- DELIVERING the presentation calls upon four of your Five Principles of Good Speaking and Communication – Be Clear, Be Simple, Be Vivid and Be Natural. Look after the main ideas and the words will look after themselves. Imagine yourself as leading your audience on an interesting, exciting and potentially fruitful journey.
- 'Fail to prepare; prepare to fail.' The best way to beat nerves is to build your confidence. The foundations for confidence are laid long before your presentation begins but you may still have to act confidently on the day.

A flame should be lighted at the commencement and kept alive with unremitting splendour to the end.
Michael Faraday, English chemist and author of
Advice to a Lecturer

9

SUCCESSFUL INTERVIEWS

'There is more wisdom in listening than speaking.'
Sudanese proverb

We can define an interview as a meeting, usually between two people, arranged with a clear purpose and with the roles of the participants well defined. The word itself comes from the French verb *s'entrevoir*, meaning 'to see each other'.

Interviews range from a meeting or conversation between a journalist or radio or television presenter and a person whose views are sought for publication or broadcasting, oral examinations of candidates for a job or place in higher education, to an interrogation of a person by the police about a specific event – sometimes euphemistically known as 'helping the police with their inquiries'. What do interviews have in common?

- They are usually prearranged, with the possible exception of the dismissal interview.
- Both interviewer and, generally, interviewee need to prepare for them.
- They all have a definite purpose, which should be clearly known to both participants.
- They all centre upon communication – 'the process by

which meanings are exchanged between people through the use of a common set of symbols'.

Most managers think that they are good at conducting interviews, just as most of us think we are good drivers. How would you assess your own ability in this respect? In fact interviewing, like driving, is an art with its advanced levels. But you don't have to be ill in order to get better. However proficient at interviewing you may believe yourself to be, there is always room for improvement.

In this chapter, I shall first remind you of some common sense points, and then move on to discuss structure, the different types of question you can use, and finally, the performance or appraisal interview. My reason for focusing upon the last is that it often poses particular communication problems. Selection interviews, for example, deal mainly with the exchange of information – about the candidate and about the job – which, from the communication point of view, is relatively straightforward. The art of judgement – choosing the right person – of which interviews are merely a part, falls outside the scope of this book, although it is a subject I hope to address later. By contrast, appraisal interviews involve the importing of praise and criticism. This can be much more emotive, and when emotions rush through the door, meaning often jumps out of the window. This type of interview does call for very good communication skills, both on the part of interviewer and the interviewee.

Because of their overtones, the words *praise* and *criticism* are now often being replaced in management jargon by the more user-friendly or neutral-sounding *feedback*. One writer, for example, talks about *affirmative feedback* and *developmental feedback*, presumably praise and criticism. Feedback, as we have seen in Chapter 1 (page 3), is a systems term by origin. It refers to a loop in which one part of a system gives information to an antecedent part so that the collective function can be improved. Giving praise and criticism are more than feedback in the strict sense of the partial reversion of the effects of a process to its source, for they are forms of teaching.

This chapter is written with you as a leader or manager in the role of interviewer in mind. But in reality you will often be the interviewee. Use your whole experience and come to understand the skill of interviewing by studying it down both ends of the telescope.

SOME GENERAL ADVICE ON INTERVIEWS

Purpose

The Communication Principle of Be Clear requires that you *both* know the purpose of this personal meeting. Are you both clear about it? What else is on the agenda? The first step is to confirm that you share a common mind on that score.

You may well have stated orally and/or in writing what you conceive to be the purpose but it is usually necessary to check that the interviewee shares your perception. Otherwise you will be talking at cross-purposes.

One way of clarifying purpose is to ask yourself – and perhaps the other person – about outcomes. What are the 'success criteria' for this interview? How will we both know that it has been successful?

Exchange of information

Be clear about what information you want and expect to receive. Equally, consider what information may be asked of you. If it is a selection interview, for example, you may be asked about pay and conditions if these have not already been communicated. You may be asked about career prospects, leadership development programmes, the nature and scope of changes in the organization, and so on. Be prepared to give honest and candid answers. Tell people the realities of the situation. Never lure them to work for you under false pretences. Putting it another way, if the information you exchange isn't true or accurate, then you are passing counterfeit notes.

Keeping control

The first responsibility of leadership is to take and keep control. As interviewer, your role is the leading one. You will be expected to guide the discussion.

Keep to the subject in hand and avoid going off in all directions. If the conversation becomes rambling and increasingly irrelevant, you will both lose sight of the aim of the interview.

Bear in mind the purpose of the interview and get to the point early on. This is especially necessary where difficult things have to be said.

Don't talk too much yourself. You are primarily in the listening role. In ordinary conversation the balance between talking and listening is roughly equivalent. But in interviewing you should aim to speak no more than about 20 per cent of the time. Most of your talking, moreover, should be in the form of questions. If you are asked information-seeking questions, confine your answers to what the interviewee needs to know.

Finally, try to stick to the time allocated. The discipline of being concise should prevent you from overrunning, providing that you have budgeted time correctly for the interview. Interviews ought to be more like sprints than marathons.

STRUCTURING THE INTERVIEW

Structuring or planning the interview is necessary if it is to avoid becoming a shapeless conversation. The amount of structure will depend upon the purpose of the interview and your own experience. The more experienced you are, the less you will need a pre-planned structure of questions to be asked. You should always, however, have a note of the main questions or issues you want to ask or raise.

Like games of chess, interviews have a beginning, middle and end. Each requires skill, as does making the transitions from one to the other. The list below may help to clarify this:

Opening
- Introduce yourself and any other important factors.
- Confirm the purpose of the meeting straight away.
- Put the other person at ease.
- Try to encourage an atmosphere where both of you are relaxed, open-minded, committed to the purpose and prepared to discuss things calmly and frankly.

Middle
- Keep your aim firmly in mind as you exchange information.
- Keep the discussion relevant, helpful and work-oriented.
- Listen, or give the other person's replies or comments your thoughtful attention.
- Listen to the person as well as what they say, and so listen with your eyes as well as your ears.
- Make sure you have covered the agenda.

Closing
- Sum up the discussion.
- Describe the action you have decided or mutually agreed upon.
- Confirm the worthwhileness of the meeting.
- Avoid ending abruptly.
- Close on a positive, if not a higher, note.

THE SKILL OF ASKING THE RIGHT QUESTION

Questions are the tools of interviewing or – more widely – of listening. The art of interviewing largely consists of asking the right questions at the right time. There are several different kinds of question, each with its pros and cons. It is useful to have them all in your repertoire, so that you don't get stuck like a broken record on only one type of question.

TYPES AND DESCRIPTIONS OF QUESTIONS		
QUESTION	USES	DISADVANTAGES
The Yes/No Question For example, '*Have you read this report?*'	Good for checking facts. Establishes where a rough balance lies quickly (e.g. 'Are you healthy?').	Can force over-simplified answers (e.g. to the question 'Are you or are you not satisfied with your job?').
The Closed Question For example, '*How long have you worked here?*'	Best where facts or data are sought. Form of question restricts answer to a limited area.	Can sound like an interrogation. Leaves little room for discussion or explanation.
The Open-ended Question For example, '*How do you see your career progressing?*'	Good for opening up the exchange and discussion of information and ideas.	May invite long and rambling answers, leading into irrelevancies.

The Leading Question For example, '*Don't you agree that you should have done that weeks ago?*'	Not very useful, unless you are trying to push someone in a certain direction.	The knowledge gained by a leading question is usually limited in value.
The Loaded Question For example, '*What do you think about the chief executive's stupid plan for expansion in Europe?*'	Limited, unless it's deliberately provocative.	A loaded question is charged with some hidden implication or underlying suggestion. It has a bias or prejudice built into it. Can blow up in your face.
The Prompt For example, '*So what did you do then?*'	Keeps things moving, guiding the interviewee in content and direction. Clarifies if the other person has not understood what you want.	Can prematurely curtail or direct an interesting reply to an open-ended question.
The Probe For example, '*What precisely was the extent of your budget responsibility in Canada?*'	Obtains more information, following through from the general to the particular.	Can make it all sound like an interrogation.
The Mirror For example, '*So you felt completely fed up at this point?*'	A reflective way of checking whether or not you have received the other person's message accurately.	Be careful that you do not introduce a slight alteration of meaning: 'No I felt rather frustrated, but not fed up.'

The What-if Question For example, *'Supposing we opened an office in the Gulf, would that interest you?'*	Making assumptions or creating situations imaginatively and asking what the interviewee would do.	Can force someone's hand or lead to unfulfilled expectations. Only yields hypothetical information.

PERFORMANCE APPRAISAL

The performance appraisal interview has as its main purpose the improvement of an individual's work contribution. As an interview, it is governed by the general principles or rules already explored. There is nothing to add on that front, except the obvious point that if you haven't set or agreed objectives some months or weeks in advance it is more difficult to hold a successful appraisal interview.

You can and should, of course, discuss interviewees' performance of the duties of their offices or jobs – what they are being paid for – but it is easier to do that if both of you know that some progressive objectives covering all or parts of the job will be under review. Somehow people are less inclined to take on board suggestions or criticisms that come 'out of the blue' and relate to a general function of their job, such as being nice to customers. In fact the giving and receiving of criticism is one of the most difficult chapters in the art of communication. Remember Adam and Eve?

> *Thus they in mutual accusation spent*
> *The fruitless hours, neither self-condemning*

Milton's evocation of the state of Adam and Eve's relationship in these words, as they were expelled from the Garden of Eden in his book *Paradise Lost* (1667), may sound echoes in an experienced manager's mind. It is all too easy for an appraisal interview, in which one person attempts to point out to another his or her shortcomings and failings, to develop into a Miltonian slanging match of attack and counter-attack, accusation and defence. Moreover, much more emphasis is now being placed on the formal appraisal interview designed to assess work performance at regular intervals. Too often the 'how to do it' handbooks on appraisal interviews only stress the formal aspects: the value of organizing and regularizing what is in fact a natural feature of good leadership. They ignore the major problems of communications in such situations; they overlook the common experience that the giving and receiving of praise or criticism come highest on the list of difficult conversations.

Here I propose to concentrate on the exchange of praise and criticism, those precious but unstable commodities that can make or break individuals, teams and even organizations. Moreover, it would be a mistake to limit the consideration of them entirely to the formal appraisal interview: we may find ourselves dealing with praise or criticism – on the sending or receiving end – at any time of the day or night and at any place, be it the boardroom or at home.

Just as a good reader makes a good book, so a good interviewee or listener makes for an effective appraisal. As the writer of the biblical *Book of Proverbs* noted:

> *He who corrects a scoffer gets himself abuse, and he who reproves a wicked man incurs injury. Do not reprove a scoffer, or he will hate you; reprove a wise man and he will love you. Give instruction to a wise man and he will be still wiser.*

A good receiver is essential if there is to be any genuine praise or constructive criticism at all.

The words 'praise' and 'appraisal' come from the Latin verb *pretiare* meaning to set a price or value on something. Thus in one of the first printed books Thomas Caxton could write: 'They praised nothing the things that were earthly.'

Our verb 'to prize' approximates it. 'Evaluating' means virtually the same as 'appraising'. Elsewhere I have suggested that *valuing* (along with analysing and synthesizing) is one of the fundamental movements of our minds: we cannot avoid doing it without an effort, and then only for very short times. Thus appraisal or evaluation lies on the trade routes of our minds quite naturally.

Praise implies a positive evaluation of worth, excellence or merit that is communicated.

In order to have value it must be given sparingly. For praise, like gold and diamonds, owes its value only to its scarcity.

Like praise, 'criticism' was originally a neutral word, and this meaning survives in the phrase 'literary criticism'. Stemming from the Greek word for a judge, it has arrived at a sense of a 'guilty' verdict, a negative evaluation. Most people are aware, however, of the distinction between *constructive* and *negative* criticism, the former being positive in tone and accompanied by practical suggestions for improvement.

Most praise and criticism is rightly directed towards performance, or what a person *does* rather than what he or she *is*. On the other hand the distinction between doing and being is a fluid one: to some extent our actions are fruits of our character, and our character is the by-product of our actions. 'The bird carries the wings, and the wings carry the bird', as the Chinese proverb says. It is fatally easy, however, to draw false conclusions about character from observations of a person's work.

As a general rule, for that reason, it is often suggested that appraisal conversations should stop short at comments about performance and eschew any reactions to character. But there are obvious exceptions to such a common sense rule. We all need a certain balance of self-esteem. That balance is always shifting. Sometimes we respect our own conduct or stance; sometimes we feel guilty and despise ourselves; sometimes we fall into bouts of self-pity. In the hours when our proper level of self-confidence is slipping, a good leader or friend may deftly and tactfully restore our sense of self-value by some more realistic and encouraging evaluation of our character. At other moments, when self-esteem is threatening to collapse into the rubble of conceit and vanity – those afflictions which eventually impair judgement and weaken relationships – a quiet word from someone who cares can restore a more balanced sense of our worth.

Because of the connecting passage between doing and being it is important to shut the door between them as firmly as possible, so that you can comment on performance without the person concerned feeling that their whole life and personality are under scrutiny. Moreover, like a medieval confessor, you should not offer appraisal unless you are willing to undergo appraisal yourself. And you should offer your comments in such a way that you maintain, restore, or enhance the other person's sense of value, which is one of our most precious possessions.

People on the receiving end of praise often exhibit what seems to be embarrassment, as if they do not know how to respond. Some social psychologists have interpreted these reactions as evidence that people sense the potential use of praise to manipulate them. Certainly the unease may be a sign that the person being praised sees through the false motives or insincerity behind the compliments. On the other hand it may be modesty at work.

Modesty is the active way that a good person responds to praise from others; the Latin word *modus* means 'a measure'.

A modest person checks the praise given against their own measure – their own being and sum of their parts and skills, as it were. If the praiser has made a mistake, and given too much credit, he or she will politely return it to the sender by pointing out the facts. For example, they might draw attention to the contribution of other people to the meritorious actions or performance. Moreover, the praiser and the praised may be operating on different measures. Thus it is a natural instinct for modest people, who have enough self-esteem already, to deflect praise to the earth like lightning, so that it does not go to their heads. And the most effective way of doing this is to share it with others.

To reject praise absolutely, however, can be an immodest act. More accurately, it is false modesty. It denies the value or truth of someone else's statement, making them into a liar or a fraud. It denies the inherent social nature of our lives: that living consists of receiving gracefully as well as giving generously. It dries up one of the natural sources of strength and gratitude in society. Above all it is phoney or unreal.

GIVING CONSTRUCTIVE CRITICISM

If it is not always easy to receive praise gracefully in the spirit in which it was intended, by common consent, it is much harder to accept criticism. Therefore it is much more difficult to criticize others well. Through experience most of us learn some common sense rules for both giving and receiving criticism, for work judged to be below the accepted or necessary standard of performance. For example, as already mentioned, most of us appreciate criticism which is followed by *constructive* suggestions on how to improve up to and beyond the required minimum standard.

We tend to assume that criticism flows downwards, as it did when we were children. But in organizations criticism flows inwards (in the form of customer complaints), upwards and sideways. The widespread use of '360° appraisal' – assessment by colleagues and team members as well as superiors – is one organizational form of that social reality.

Whether inwards, downwards, upwards or sideways, criticism often takes the form of *complaint*. Complaining is the act of finding fault with your circumstances or treatment. It may be a justified or unjustified dissatisfaction. When you complain you are expressing in words your grief, pain or discontent. It may lead on to a formal accusation or charge.

Most complaints about someone's work imply a gap between expectation and performance. Where the complainer is ignorant of how the gap can be bridged, a mere complaint is all that can be expected from him or her. For example, you may complain to the doctor if the medicine prescribed actually makes you worse; you can hardly nominate an alternative. In appraising the work of those who report to you, however, you ought to be able to offer constructive criticism, that is with some suggestions on how the work can be improved. If you cannot do that it is doubtful whether or not you have the right to lead or manage.

Here are some ground rules for easing difficult conversations. With experience you may modify, or even occasionally omit, one or more of them – providing you know what you are doing. Can you add to the list?

Offer criticisms in private if possible, and do not spread them unnecessarily

Any effective criticism may sting a little. Your indifference to your colleague's feelings, displayed by a willingness to criticize in front of others, will be taken at least as seriously as the content of what you say. In fairness to him or her, and yourself, wait until you are alone.

Avoid long or predictable preambles

Avoid prefaces such as 'Listen. There's something I've wanted to tell you for a long time. It may hurt you, but . . .' In these matters it is best to come to the point without beating the daylights out of the proverbial bush. Nor should criticisms be invariably prefaced by positive evaluations which contain very little supplementary information, such as 'You are doing a fine job, but . . .' Don't use insincere praise as a sweetener. 'He who praises everybody praises nobody,' wrote the English author Samuel Johnson. But of course criticism will always be more readily received if you can preface it with some genuine and evidence-based praise.

Keep it as simple and as accurate as possible

Avoid overload. Try to make only one or two major criticisms at a time, rather than presenting a list of sixty or seventy! Criticisms should not be allowed to pile up. Too many major and minor points thrown together reduce clarity and are ineffective, because no one can handle that amount of critical comment. As the Chinese proverb says: 'Do not use a hatchet to remove a fly from your friend's forehead'. Nor should the simple point be endlessly repeated. The reward for good listening ought to be exemption from hearing the same shortcoming discussed again.

Exaggerations intended for emphasis, signalled by such words as *always* and *never*, rob you of your accuracy and the psychological advantages that go with it. Moreover, instead of statements such as, 'You are very idle,' it may be usually more accurate to say, 'You give me the impression of being lazy.' For that 'impression' at least is an objective fact. And if more than one person has formed that impression it should have some weight.

Offer only constructive criticism of actions that can be changed

'No man, by taking thought, can add one cubit to his stature,' as the saying goes. It is useless to criticize people for characteristics that they cannot change. Such personal remarks should be avoided. Whether or not characteristics fall into this category is a matter of judgement. After all, someone once defined character as what you have done with your personality.

Don't compare the person's behaviour with that of others

Comparisons are especially odious in appraisal conversations. No one wants to be described as inferior. Comparisons predispose others not to listen, even when the criticism or complaint is justified.

Don't talk about other people's motives when making a complaint or criticism

Motives stand closer to the inner person than his or her actions, and to pass judgement on them can be interpreted as a censure of the whole person.

Moreover, actions are often multi-motivated, and it is fatally easy for an observer to draw the wrong conclusions about these hidden springs of behaviour, especially when the interviewee is only dimly aware of why he or she does or does not do certain things. Don't confuse consequence and intention.

Always be able to back up your observations with some evidence or data. Thus an appraisal should never stray far from the facts. Avoid amateur psychology.

After making a criticism in good faith, don't apologize for it

Apology may fuel some inner doubt as to whether or not you had the right to say what you did. It is asking the other person to brace you against the stress of criticizing him or her. It imposes an unnecessary burden on them. An apologetic tone and embarrassed manner does neither of you any good. You do need moral courage. But by all means apologize if it transpires that you have got the facts wrong. It is more fitting to thank the person concerned for listening to your criticism or complaint.

In summary, giving constructive criticism is never going to be easy. If you can avoid having to do so that is an advantage. One useful strategy is to encourage interviewees to appraise themselves. For where possible, people should be encouraged to be self-critical – critical of their own performance and motivated to improve. This approach goes a long way to remove the unnecessary conflict from the meeting. Your role then becomes one of modifying, supplementing or pointing up that self-criticism as a prelude to action.

'No man can tell another his faults so as to benefit him, unless he loves him,' said American clergyman and abolitionist Henry Ward Beecher. Love, in the sense of taking the other person's interests seriously, stands here at the core of good communication.

ON THE RECEIVING END

'A blind man will not thank you for a looking-glass,' says one eighteenth-century English proverb. Assuming you are not blind in the inward eyes, however, you should work with your critic to identify the area for improvement, like a fellow surgeon working around an operating table. What should matter to both of you is any improvement in your common work. Nor will you be distracted by imperfections in your appointed (or self-appointed) critic: truth is truth whether it comes from the mouths of angels or barmaids. Try to be grateful in advance for what you are about to receive. The following tips could help:

Be quiet while you are being criticized and make it clear that you are listening

Whether you agree or not is an issue to be discussed later. Look directly at the person talking to you. Only thus can you convey that you are open to what he or she is saying. Gazing out of the window is not so convincing!

Under no condition find fault with the person who has just criticized you

If he or she has used the wrong words or got a minor fact wrong, do not overreact, wait half an hour. If you counter-attack by reciprocating the criticism – 'Now I think about it, you come late to meetings too' – this implies that you interpret it as an insult. Or you become so busy in marshalling your own forces for the attack that you neglect to heed what is actually being said.

Don't create the impression that the other person is destroying your spirit

Some people can be belligerent at first, and then start acting as though they were at the edge of despair. Don't try to manipulate the appraiser by appearing completely defeated.

Don't try to change the subject

Humour is a way of keeping matters in proportion but a flippant reaction suggests that a person cannot take criticism seriously. Changing the subject is a more extreme form of taking flight from the issue. Use your mind to help articulate the objection, not to make it disappear.

Don't caricature the complaint

If a person says you were *thoughtless*, don't ascribe to them the statement that you are irresponsible and then defend yourself against a charge that has not been made. The deliberate exaggeration of a charge against you is a tactic for avoiding it.

Don't assume that your critic has some ulterior, hostile motive

Take the criticism at face value. The question about the interviewer's motives should come later, if at all.

Convey to the other person that you understand his or her objection

Paraphrasing or using a minor question is one good way of doing this. In effect you are saying that the message is received and noted.

Don't let people get at you on the pretext that they are giving you constructive criticism. You have the right at any time, I believe, to turn off the tap of criticism. Refusal to allow you to do so suggests a compulsive critic at work. If you are out to beat a dog you're sure to find a stick. The path is narrow: you must be open to criticism but subject it to examination before accepting it.

To receive criticism well and to act upon it is the ultimate badge of the good listener. If it is unjustified, as later certified by completely impartial 'appeal judges', the appraisal interview can still be creatively turned into an occasion for learning humility.

If you feel that the criticism is fully justified, or at least that there is something in it for further reflection, thank your critics for their time and effort. 'Take each man's censure, but reserve your judgement,' as William Shakespeare puts it in *Hamlet*. They have done you a personal favour; they have given you a present. 'Criticism is a study by which people grow more important and formidable at very small expense,' concluded the writer Samuel Johnson. Can you afford to ignore such valuable and free tuition?

How do you handle criticism?

An advice columnist once wrote that 'The best way to measure people is to watch the way they behave when you offer them something for free.'

I think you can tell even more about people by how they react when you offer them criticism.

People generally respond to criticism, constructive or otherwise, in four stages.

1. They ignore it
This is the response of dullards and incompetents. They have no idea what you're talking about, why you're telling them, or

what they can do about it. They have no business being in your company.

2. They deny it

This is often a sign of a dangerously selective mind. You have to wonder what else this person is leaving out in his dealings outside the company and in his communications within.

3. They deflect it

This is the response of the master politician. When he's on the spot, he always seems to know more about what everyone else is (or is not) doing than he knows about himself. Quite often, he doesn't even realize he's blaming others for his failings. That makes it vital that you do.

4. They accept it

This is a sign of emotional maturity. The people who can accept responsibility for a problem – whether they're directly at fault or not – are generally the only people who can correct it.

The people I admire – and prefer to hire – progress the first three stages very quickly.

Mark McCormack, *Business Age*, 1992

THE TOUCHSTONE OF EFFECTIVENESS

Sometimes there will be an immediate negative reaction against a justified criticism, even a rejection of it. Later, however, an observer might see that the person concerned is actually working in a different and improved way. Consciously the criticism and the 'critic' have been rejected; unconsciously, or in the depth mind, the message has been hoisted in and transformed into action. In such instances the appraiser will receive no credit, no reward of gratitude from the other person. But leadership does not entitle one to such rewards. Anyway, the proportion of those people who are likely to return thanks for such personal help is probably no more than about one in ten.

It may be useful to the appraiser to recall that he or she is addressing a person's subconscious or depth mind through the gateways of the senses. And it sometimes takes time for the penny to drop, as we say. A second or third interview or conversation may become necessary, for repetition on different occasions, couched in other words and images, may implant a message more firmly. Yet the balance is fine. We have to guard always 'the sacred right of rejection'. If the message is repeatedly rejected then the appraiser has to reconsider his advice. It may be possible to accept the differences of opinion bravely. On the other hand, the interviewee's prospects or even very employment may rest upon their acceptance of the proposed improvement. If this is so, it is of course essential that this is made absolutely clear during the interview or course of interviews with some deadlines also clearly set out.

The good leader uses his or her power of praising or criticizing judiciously to achieve good purposes, while building up the community and forwarding the growth of individuals. With regard to the latter, he might well meditate occasionally on the prayer of the Psalmist, 'Let the righteous rather smite me friendly: and reprove me. But let not their precious balms break my head,' or some similar saying.

This consideration of the difficulties of giving and receiving of both praise and criticism leads us back to the centrality for good communication of integrity, both in its professional and personal senses. Integrity is the quality that makes people trust one another. It is the bedrock on which a lasting relationship can be built, one that can take the exchange of meanings, however unpalatable, because the end is to edify or build you up. As management guru Peter Drucker said in *The Practice of Management* (1956):

> When all is said and done, developing men still requires a basic quality in the manager which cannot be created by supplying skills or by emphasizing the importance of the task. It requires integrity of character . . . It may be argued that every occupation – the doctor, the lawyer, the grocer – requires integrity. But there is a difference. The manager lives with the people he manages, he decides what their work is to be, he directs it, he trains them for it, he appraises it and, often, he decides their future. The relationship of merchant and client requires honourable dealings. Being a manager, though, is more like being a parent, or a teacher. And in these relationships honourable dealings are not enough; personal integrity is of the essence.

KEY POINTS: SUCESSFUL INTERVIEWS

- Interviews or personal meetings – usually between two people – are an integral part of professional life. They can be classified according to their purpose but they share in common certain characteristics: they are usually pre-arranged, require preparation and a definite purpose, and the people involved participate in well-defined roles.
- The principles of clarity, preparation, simplicity, natural-ness and conciseness should inform or govern the exchange of information and meaning that lies at the core of an interview. Together, they spell effectiveness.
- As an interviewer you are in the lead role. You have to take charge in a pleasant but firm way and guide the dis-cussion to a clear and successful conclusion, if possible for both parties.

- There are few techniques in interviewing that really matter, beyond the ability to keep your mouth shut for as much of the time as possible. But you should develop the skill of both knowing the range of possible questions and choosing the right one at the right time, like a carpenter selecting just the best chisel for a particular job.
- Giving praise and criticism in relation to performance isn't easy, which is why many appraisal interviews are such unsatisfactory affairs. By applying and practising the ground rules listed in this chapter you can make a significant improvement in your effectiveness as an appraiser.
- But can you take criticism yourself? Again this chapter has listed some common sense guidelines for getting the best out of being appraised. Look upon your next performance appraisal as not a threat but an opportunity.

The deepest principle in human nature is the craving to be appreciated.

William James, US psychologist and philosopher

10

LEADING
EFFECTIVE MEETINGS

*'If people are of one heart, even the
yellow earth can become gold.'*
Chinese proverb

'Nothing is impossible until it is sent to a committee,' said
one manager in a large organization somewhat despairingly
at a recent conference on innovation. Meetings proliferate but
they have acquired a bad name for ineffectiveness, time wasting and sheer lack of fun. So said the witches in Shakespeare's
Macbeth:

> *When shall we three meet again*
> *In thunder, lightning, or in rain?*

Managers will certainly meet in better conditions than those
witches on their blasted heath but they definitely know that
they will be meeting again – and again!

Meeting is a very general word that encompasses any
situation in which two or more people come together by
accident or design, in an encounter that may be momentary
or prolonged. Almost all of them involve some form of

communication. But the meetings that concern us in this chapter are those that involve a group of people met for discussion. How do you lead or manage that discussion effectively?

THE ROLE OF DISCUSSION

Discussion suggests to some a rambling or freewheeling conversation in which people express their views or sentiments to each other – just the sort of thing to be banned from efficient, tightly controlled and brisk meetings! But, rightly understood, discussion lies at the core of all purposeful meetings. It should be differentiated from conversation on the one hand and a formal debate on the other. It ought to be limited to a given theme. More often than not, discussion is a way of reaching conclusions or determining a course of action.

The actual word 'discussion' comes from a Latin root that means 'to shake apart'. Possibilities are sifted or shaken apart. Their pros and cons are considered. For this work to be done effectively, five ingredients need to be present:

- *Planning* in advance is essential to successful discussion. It is futile to rely upon spontaneous combustion to develop profitable talk. The initiative for this planning may be taken by a designated leader but it is better when at least some members of the group can work on it together.

- *Informality* is desirable to encourage the fullest possible participation, although the size of the group or audience and the seating arrangements in the meeting place impose some limits. Organized informality best describes this objective.

- *Participation* is an essential ingredient of good discussion, for this method assumes that each individual may have something of value to contribute and that the cooperative pooling of all available information is the best way to find the right solution. In small groups everyone who wishes to may speak; in a large public discussion only a few can get the floor but it should be emphasized that active listening is participation.

- *Purpose* is essential in good discussion. Merely pleasant or socially useful talk that skips from one topic to another is not discussion as conceived here.

- *Leadership* in some form is necessary for a successful discussion. In public meetings, the leader or chairman may be assisted by a secretary or PA. In small groups, whose members know each other, the functions of leadership may sometimes be shared by various individuals.

The seating plan

The leader's responsibility for planning starts before the meeting in question begins. By using common sense, laced with some visual imagination, he or she should be able to foresee what will be required in or near the place of meeting. In particular they ought to look at the seating arrangements, because sometimes these can impose their own (often unwelcome) pattern on the exchange of information and ideas, as one of King James I's chief ministers, Francis Bacon, observed over three hundred years ago:

A long table and a square table, or seats about the walls, seem things of form, but are things of substance; for at a long table a few at the upper end, in effect, sway all the

business; but in the other form there is more use of the counsellors' opinions that sit lower. A king, when he presides in council, let him beware how he opens his own inclination too much in that which he propounds; for else counsellors will but take the wind of him, and, instead of giving free counsel, will sing him a song of 'I shall please'.

The varieties of discussion, private and public, are endless. But, as a rule, the general purpose of the meeting, the size of the group, and its progress in analysing the problem, should determine the form of discussion used in a particular situation. A *committee*, for example, is a small group, appointed by the parent organization, which meets to investigate a problem and, later, to formulate its report and recommendation. At a *conference*, by contrast, delegates representing various organizations, sometimes cooperative, sometimes hostile, meet to consider a problem and, if possible, to recommend a joint course of action. At other times a conference – alias a workshop or seminar – may have as its only purpose the acquiring of new knowledge or skills by those taking part.

The terms *leader* and *chairman* are used almost interchangeably by writers on meetings. There is a tendency, however, to speak of a *leader* of an informal group discussion and a *chairman* of a committee, conference or public meeting – the more formal occasions. *Chair* or *chairperson* is now sometimes substituted for the latter in the interests of 'political correctness' but most people are still happy with *chairman*, for *man* is a synonym for humanity as well as the name of one of its two constituent sexes.

If you are a manager, it follows that you will probably have to chair meetings in the formal sense and also lead discussion. These roles are occasionally separated but more often they go hand in hand. It is not always easy to combine them, for it is like being both a football referee and the captain of a side at the same time.

BE CLEAR ABOUT PURPOSE

Discussion can serve a variety of purposes. Even within a single meeting it may change gear from one to another. Here are some of these general purposes:

- To exchange information
- To make decisions
- To release tensions
- To form attitudes
- To instruct or teach

These purposes are not mutually exclusive. Pooling available information, for example, often precedes and accompanies decision making. It may relieve tension! Again, as another example, early research in this field suggests that those who gain the most information through discussion are most likely to change their attitudes.

BE PREPARED BEFORE THE MEETING

The general purpose of the meeting needs to be broken down into more tangible aims – directional but open-ended – and more specific objectives or targets. Once more the Communication Principle of Be Prepared comes into play as you begin to think ahead and plan the meeting in more detail. For careful preparation is the secret of success.

The *agenda* is a key factor. It shouldn't be just a list of headings to jog your memory during a meeting. Draw it up with thought, indicating whether an item is for discussion or decision. Briefly describe the matter or subject. 'Mounting costs', for example, looks too brief and vague, whereas 'Mounting costs: to discuss the report on energy conservation in the factory and make decisions on the first and third recommendations on p. 16' is much more definite. It gives people the opportunity to think about the matter beforehand. Ensure that everyone receives the agenda and relevant papers – in this case the 'Energy Conservation Report' – at least five clear days before the meeting.

People take in information more readily through their eyes than their ears. Visual aids should therefore play a part in your meetings more often than not: if they are clear, simple and vivid they can save you time.

Time spent on preparation is seldom wasted. If you go into a meeting clear about the objectives, having thought about the subject in advance and with everything ready, it is already most probable that your meeting will be effective.

CHECKLIST:
PREPARING FOR DISCUSSION

	Yes	No
Are you clear about the purpose of this planned discussion?	☐	☐
Do the other participants know that purpose?	☐	☐
If not, do you plan to communicate it to them before the meeting?	☐	☐
Have you circulated any necessary information well before the meeting?	☐	☐
Have you identified the main topics to be discussed? Is each objective clear?	☐	☐

Have you framed some questions to stimulate discussion?	☐	☐
Have you prepared a timetable for the meeting?	☐	☐
Is the accommodation and seating plan arranged?	☐	☐
Are all necessary materials, including visual aids and flipcharts, ready?	☐	☐

GUIDING THE DISCUSSION

As a chairman yourself it is useful to bear in mind that you have two principal functions within your role. Being chairman in the narrow sense means you are accountable for seeing that procedures are adhered to and that participants both behave themselves and contribute as effectively as possible to the business in hand. You are there to see fair play, to ensure that everyone has their turn and to apply the appropriate rules, not unlike a referee. The foreman of a jury is a chairman in this specific sense.

Secondly, you may be the group's leader or manager as well, charged with achieving specified results. The nature of those outcomes will necessarily vary according to the type of meeting. In creative-thinking meetings, for example, the leader's role may be more that of a catalyst than traffic controller.

There can be some obvious tensions between the 'referee' and 'leader' roles. Some groups and leaders indeed seek to avoid them by appointing a referee-type chairman, like the Speaker in the House of Commons, leaving leaders free to argue their case in the meeting without having to preside over it. Other chairmen signal when they are changing hats by 'stepping down from the chair' for a particular item on the agenda.

In most situations it makes sense for the chairman to exercise both functions. There is some overlap between the roles anyway. Let us assume here that you are doing both.

Some of the key leadership functions, such as *defining the task* and *planning*, have been discussed above. But as chairman you should remember to begin the meeting by saying what the purpose is and why it is necessary. Don't assume that everyone knows. You may also want to check that the participants are comfortable with the agenda, so that *your* plan for the meeting now becomes *our* plan for it. In a pleasant but firm way, show that you have taken charge.

Once work has started on the agenda you will have to exercise the function of *controlling*, which should be done with intelligence and sensitivity. What would you do about an over-talkative person? It is essential to stop him but it has to be done tactfully as well as firmly: 'Thank you, Michael, I think we have got the drift of your argument. Susan, you haven't said anything yet. Do you agree with Michael or not?'

Experienced colleagues at a discussion meeting will seldom require you to exercise this *gate-keeping* function of 'opening the door' for someone to make a contribution beyond listening intently. More often than not, your energies will be deployed in shutting the door! But as a leader you should always be aware of who hasn't contributed, and if you think that diffidence or lack of assertiveness to jump into the busy pool is the reason, you can at least offer an opportunity for speaking.

If a long-winded person still challenges you for the right of way – by continuing to talk over others or by interrupting again – then you will have to show more steel until the message is taken. Never lose control.

Heading off potential or actual irrelevancies is also a vital part of controlling a meeting. Sometimes a 'red herring' looks more 'tasty' than the 'bread-and-butter' items on the agenda. Where the object of a meeting is creative thinking, as in brainstorming sessions, it is often worth pursuing red herrings, for the apparently irrelevant may disguise the germ of a new idea.

The problems of controlling or guiding a discussion are heightened by the fact that it is in the nature of the beast to ramble and become discursive. As the model below suggests, the complex pattern of lines of communication available in a group situation – as opposed to a one-to-one interview – makes control that much more difficult. Some formal groups, in the parliamentary tradition, try to solve that potential difficulty by making it a rule that all remarks should be made to and through the chairman. That may work in more formal debate, especially if it involves a large number of people, but it is antithetical to the more informal and group-centred nature of discussion.

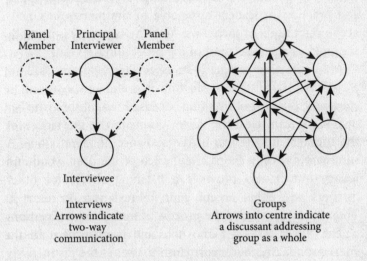

Lines of communication

To exercise these leadership functions and to contribute to the discussion, you will need to develop yourself by becoming:

- A clear and rapid thinker
- An attentive listener
- Able to express yourself clearly and succinctly
- Ready to clarify views badly expressed
- Able to be impartial and impersonal
- A preventer of inappropriate interruptions
- Patient, tolerant and kind
- Friendly but brisk and businesslike

One important way of guiding the discussion is to *summarize* progress so far, so that the remaining agenda or issues stand out clearly. Thus a summary given during a meeting – rather than in conclusion – can act as a trumpet sounding the recall. But the summary has to be accurate. With all their other responsibilities it requires a high level of natural ability and practice for leaders to be able to summarize succinctly at the right time, in such a way that the summary is instantly accepted as a true account of the proceedings to date.

Although *summarizing* is an especially important skill for a chairman, all listeners can find it useful on occasions. A summary is a sign of listening because it establishes whether or not you can select the salient points to the satisfaction of the speaker and the rest of the audience, if there is one. A summary not only chops away much of the dead wood and foliage but it also provides a listening check, for other listeners will either accept your abbreviation or reject it. Thus a summary helps the process of thought and digestion.

The singer takes a piano note and transforms it into a vocal sound. Another chairmanship asset is the distinctively human ability to *interpret* from one language into another, without loss of fidelity to the original. The interpreter must be able to divine meaning and translate it into a different language. For example, the contribution of a technical specialist may have to be translated into language simple enough to be understood with reasonable effort around the table. Your ability to do so will test your powers as a listener. But such a timely interpretation can contribute to the overall direction of the discussion.

Your manner may do as much if not more than your words to encourage – or discourage – genuine communication. Humour, modesty and firmness have their own part to play. As the leader's own task encompasses the creation of a warm, friendly but businesslike atmosphere, it is vital that you should check whether or not your manner aids and abets in promoting good communication. In the right time and place, ask for feedback on this score.

If someone is asked to take action as a result of discussion on an item, the chairman should check that the participant understands and accepts that action. Steps or actions thus agreed should normally carry a completion time.

The question as to whether a committee – a decision making or problem-solving group – can be executive, that is it can do anything on its own, is really trivial. Literally as a body it can no more do anything than a football team can score a goal. In each case there must be an individual agent but it is the group that makes it possible for the individual to act. Although its decision will in most cases be carried out by one of its members or its officers, in a real sense the action is the action of the committee. The important decision has been made by the committee, or is a consequence of its deliberations.

The effective chairman

The Prime Minister shouldn't speak too much himself in Cabinet. He should start the show or ask somebody else to do so, and then intervene only to bring out the more modest chaps who, despite their seniority, might say nothing if not asked. And the Prime Minister must sum up ... Particularly when a non-Cabinet minister is asked to attend, especially if it is his first time, the Prime Minister may have to be cruel. The visitor may want to show how good he is, and go on too long. A good thing is to take no chance and ask him to send the Cabinet a paper in advance ... If somebody else looks like making a speech, it is sound to nip in with, 'Are you *objecting*? You're not? Right. Next business', and the Cabinet can move on leaving in its wake a trail of clear, crisp uncompromising decisions. That is what government is about. And the challenge to democracy is to get it done quickly.

Clement Attlee, former UK Prime Minister

Remember that discussion is a slow process. It is inappropriate when quick action is required. Nor has it much value in problem solving if group members lack relevant knowledge or information. Moreover, the informality inherent in discussion means that it is no substitute for a comprehensive statement of all the issues or a sustained presentation of an argument. Lastly, the prospect of discussion seldom encourages thorough or meticulous preparation compared to, say, if you were asked to give a presentation. The results may be poor-quality thinking and inadequate decisions.

These limitations of discussion should not be made into an excuse to dispense with it or to cut it down to the bare minimum. Leadership can hardly be democratic if there is no discussion. They only emphasize the necessity for its *intelligent* use, on the right kinds of topics and problems, after adequate planning, and under optimum conditions of leadership and teamwork.

Good chairmanship is vital for effective meetings. The chairman's task will sometimes pose problems, but a good chairman can make sure that a meeting is punctual, covers the ground, keeps moving forward and makes the appropriate decisions. Beneath that process lies purposeful communication.

KEY POINTS: LEADING EFFECTIVE MEETINGS

Here, by way of summary, are ten commandments for managing communication in groups:

- Keep the objectives of all meetings clearly in mind.
- Plan meetings carefully – decide who is to be present, circulate the agenda and any relevant information in advance.
- Ensure that all, and only, the necessary people are present.
- Agree time limits in advance, and start on time. Try to hold the meetings in a room with a clock.
- Plan the agenda carefully, allocating specific amounts of time to each item. Include time to establish the aims of the meeting, ensure effective discussion, reach conclusions and agree the necessary actions.
- Ensure that, when minutes are necessary, these are concise and definite, and include reference to who is to do what, and by when.
- End meetings on a positive note, summarizing decisions taken and action to be implemented.
- Remember, as chairman, to blend the two roles of referee and leader.

- Analyse your performance as chairman regularly and be prepared to solicit feedback so that you can develop your skills.
- Review regular meetings from time to time. Make sure that they are necessary and that the right people are there.

> *But of a good leader, who talks little,*
> *When his work is done, his aim fulfilled,*
> *They will all say, 'We did this ourselves.'*
> Lao Tzu, Chinese Taoist philosopher

11

COMMUNICATING IN ORGANIZATIONS

'The first function of the executive is to develop
and maintain a system of communication.'
*Chester Barnard, US business executive and
management expert*

Large human organizations are rarely created at a stroke
of the pen. They tend to evolve organically from working
groups or teams, which in turn come about through the
leadership of one or two people.

A team is an organization in microcosm. It is a whole made
up of interdependent parts, each with its proper function,
evolved to achieve a purpose that one person could not attain
alone or unaided. The 'parts' in this case are other individuals.

In an organization, the 'parts' are themselves teams or
workgroups. Often the transition from working group to
larger organization is by a process of rapid or slow organic
growth. Consider this quote from A. A. Milne's *The House
at Pooh Corner* (1928):

It was just the day for Organizing Something, or for
Writing a Notice signed Rabbit ... It was a Captainish

sort of day, when everybody said 'Yes, Rabbit' and 'No, Rabbit' and waited until he had told them.

At some stage or another, 'Rabbits' are employed to give the 'Something' that has evolved some systematic arrangement or organization. The critical factor here is the identification or creation of a hierarchy. 'It was a Captainish sort of day . . .'

Often organizers out to bring order into relative chaos do have some predetermined scheme in mind, such as the military system. But the military system merely reflects a more primitive or natural method of social ordering in large groups, which can be expressed as a simple model:

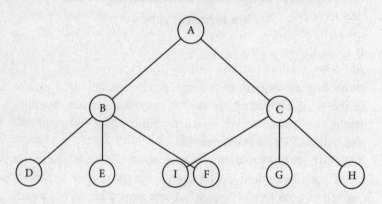

Elementary hierarchy

In the 'Elementary hierarchy' diagram above, A has overall leadership responsibility. Three team leaders – D, E, F, G, H and I – report directly to B and C, who report in turn directly to A. All the elements of hierarchy are here. We have some rather cumbersome Latin-based words – subordinate, coordinate and superordinate – to describe where people come in the structure or order thus created:

Subordinates   B and C are subordinate to A; all the others are subordinate to B and C as well; and the team members in each of the six groups are subordinate to their leaders, and all above.

Coordinates   B and C are coordinate with each other, as are D, E, F, G, H and I. Team members are also coordinates within teams.

Superordinates   are all the named leaders, A being the ultimate superordinate at the top of the pyramid.

Although 'hierarchy' comes from the Greek word for a ruling body of priests organized into orders or ranks, each priest subordinate to the one above it, it sounds in English like 'higherarchy', a system where some are higher and some are lower than others. This UP–DOWN metaphor is very strong. It gives us, for example, the idea of several horizontal *levels* of responsibility, each accompanied (eventually if not immediately) by rank and status.

Notice that hierarchy (or higherarchy) runs counter to tribal life where people are on the same level as their leader and there are no interpositions of other levels. The tribal structure looks more like this:

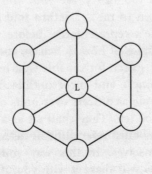

The tribal structure

In a Bedouin tribe, for example, the sheikh pitches his tent in the middle, and keeps an open door to all-comers. Members of the tribe are essentially free and equal, although in larger tribes there were sub-groups of families or kin. Yet all have the right to take complaints or problems to the paramount sheikh for arbitration or solution.

Originally we were all tribal and the tribal tradition has been deeply influential. For example, it is the matrix of modern democracy. When then has the hierarchical organization prevailed? Sheer size as tribes multiply into nations was one reason. The other reason was military necessity. Armed tribal hordes turned into disciplined armies only as and when they accepted the principle of hierarchy.

Organizing the people

One day, while the tribes of Israel were in the desert, Jethro saw his son-in-law Moses sitting alone with people standing around him from morning till evening, counselling them and solving disputes.

'This is not the best way to do it,' said Jethro. 'You will only wear yourself out and wear out all the people who are here. The task is too heavy for you; you cannot do it by yourself. Now listen to me . . .' Jethro told him that he must remain the people's representative before God and instruct them in the principles of how to behave and what to do. 'But you must yourself search for capable God-fearing men among all the people, honest and incorruptible men, and appoint them over the people as officers over units of a thousand, of a hundred, of fifty or ten. They shall sit as a permanent court for the people; they must refer difficult cases to you but decide simple cases themselves. In this way your burden will be lightened, and they will share it with you. If you do this, God will give you strength, and you will be able to go on. And, moreover, this whole people will here and now regain peace and harmony.'

Two strands have become confused in this Biblical story: the establishment of a court of justice and organization for military purposes.

It follows that 'civilized' nations such as the Greeks and Romans, who were willing to subject themselves to the discipline of organizations, could conquer tribes or tribal federations in battle. The Roman Army is still the copybook example or model of a very large organization.

Formal communication

Now with a small group or team as a leader you can communicate by informal personal contact. But organization implies that you communicate through formal channels, such as a military chain of command. A corollary is that if you work in organizations you have to respect these formal channels.

That doesn't mean to say that *informal* communication is totally absent from organizations – that is far from the case. There is plenty of information discussion, conversation and networking in most organizations. But they should be essentially supplementary. If informal communication dominates it is probably because the formal communication system – the core of the organization – isn't working well.

In the context of an organization, *size* and *geographical spread* always put a strain on its power to communicate effectively. If *rapid change* is thrown into the equation the situation can be worse. For conditions of change call for better communication, whereas size, geographical spread and elements of change itself are working against you.

To overcome the potential problems you need a practical philosophy of communication that embraces the *content* of communication, the *directions* it must take, and your *personal responsibility*. As we explore these three aspects bear in mind the model of the Communication Star (see page 20).

CONTENT

If you are familiar with the 'Three Circles' model or general theory of teams and organizations you have a ready-made definition of what people need or want as far as communication is concerned. Let me briefly remind you of the model:

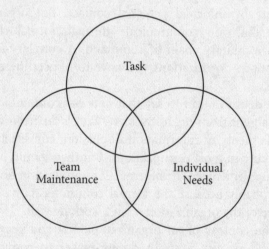

The Three Circles

According to the theory, there are three areas of need present in working groups and organizations:

- To achieve the common task
- To be held together or to maintain themselves as cohesive unities
- The needs which individuals bring with them into the group

The main *content* of communication – information, ideas and knowledge, for example – in your organization should tie in with these three overlapping areas. Here I am concentrating on communication inside 'the egg' – the safe confines of the office, business or company. Of course, members of any organization will be communicating outside 'the egg' as well, to customers, clients, suppliers and the public in some shape or form. The internal communication needs are as follows:

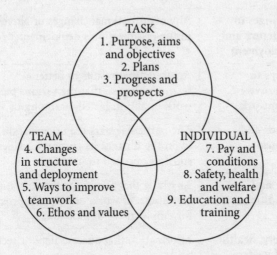

TASK
1. Purpose, aims and objectives
2. Plans
3. Progress and prospects

TEAM
4. Changes in structure and deployment
5. Ways to improve teamwork
6. Ethos and values

INDIVIDUAL
7. Pay and conditions
8. Safety, health and welfare
9. Education and training

Communication content in three circles

CONTENT OF COMMUNICATION	
AREA	**NOTES**
1 **Purpose, aim and objectives**	The core *purpose*, the key *aims* and the more tangible *objectives* of the organization are central in communication. Purpose answers the question 'Why?'
2 **Plans and policies**	Planning answers the questions 'What?', 'When?', 'How?', 'Where?' and 'Who?'. Planning may be at strategic, operational or team levels.
3 **Progress and prospects**	Progress motivates – prospects motivate even more This could include new products, innovations and positive changes in the pipeline.
4 **Changes in structure and deployment**	Any organizational changes or alterations in the organization's deployment.
5 **Ways to improve teamwork**	Anything that results in better teamworking, so that the various parts work in an integrated, harmonious whole.
6 **Ethos and values**	The particular stars the organization steers by in the form of its corporate values; its spirit as opposed to its form.
7 **Pay and conditions**	Anything that affects the remuneration, conditions of work, or personal prospects for employment of individuals.
8 **Safety, health and welfare**	Information that affects safety or security.
9 **Education and training**	Whatever may contribute to the personal development – present competence and future capability – of each individual member.

The list opposite is indicative not exhaustive but it covers the guts of what people working in organizations both need to know and expect to know. People look out for a vision to inspire their work, a sense of belonging to an interdependent and high-performance team and for information that improves their sense of value as individuals in this large organization.

Share your information

Poor leaders hold on to information as a source of power and control. As Jan Carlson, former Chief Executive of Scandinavian Airlines once said: 'An individual without information cannot take responsibility. An individual with information cannot help but take responsibility.' Good leaders see the value in sharing information to improve decision making.

DIRECTIONS OR FLOWS

Communication is more than words: it is the imparting of meaning – voluntarily or involuntarily – and it flows.

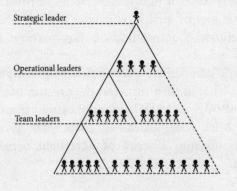

Three levels of leadership

The most obvious direction of flow is DOWNWARDS from the top to the bottom, or, if you prefer it, from the CENTRE to the PERIPHERY. Imagine a military command post, for example, where the general briefs his commanders, who in turn brief their captains. There are three levels of leadership at work here: *strategic*, *operational* and *team*.

You can see that there is a formal communication structure in place to transmit and translate the general's battle plan into action.

In the past, however, the above 'Three Levels of Leadership' system has not been so good for UPWARDS communication. What you may ask does a common soldier have to say to a general anyway? The answer was not much. Better armies and navies did introduce constitutional systems for the upward transmission of grievances – never easy because your immediate superior was often the source of your grievance and had no interest in passing your complaints upwards! In Nelson's enlightened navy, for example, every sailor had the right to approach an admiral directly and make a verbal or written complaint or grievance.

What has changed out of all recognition is the nature of operations. Now everyone has the responsibility of passing upwards any relevant information about, for instance, product performance or quality, customer needs or the responses of competitors. Communication has become a two-way traffic.

The same competitive pressures have put a premium on teamwork. That in turn sorts out the organizations that have gone SIDEWAYS, or lateral communications from those who still have brick walls instead of chalk lines, dividing them like bulkheads into a series of watertight departments or businesses.

YOUR RESPONSIBILITY AS A LEADER

Change throws up the need for leaders; leaders tend to create change. So never complain about change if you are a leader: it is what you are there for! It isn't all about change, however, for you have to balance it against the interests of continuity. So that calls for judgement on the direction, scope and pace of change.

Leadership and communication cannot be separate either. Can you think of a good leader who is not a good communicator? Therefore it is leadership that stitches together the needs for effective change and good communication.

The first step is to see yourself in a role that requires DOWNWARDS, UPWARDS and SIDEWAYS communication. Even as a strategic leader, you need to be able to communicate upwards to the board of directors or its equivalent. The content of what you communicate should always be relatable to 'The Three Circles' (see diagram on page 202). Some of it will be self-generated – your vision, your ideas or your plans. But much of your work will be as a channel of communication for information coming from other sources that you have a duty to pass on by virtue of your appointment. How should you do it?

As a general principle, the *high-priority information should go by the best method of communication, which is face-to-face backed by writing*.

As a leading insurance broker once told me: 'It is no accident that for hundreds of years the basic method of transacting business in markets has been face-to-face confrontation between the principals subsequently ratified by written contract, because by this method one can achieve the three criteria of good communication, namely that it should be clear, quick and include a response. It is a personal contact and relationships which count, and the market system would not operate without it.' As trust declines, so does communication at this level.

You should develop an unerring sense both of priorities – Aneurin Bevan, Welsh Labour politician and one of the chief architects of the NHS, once said that '75 per cent of politics is priorities – and the most appropriate methods for their communication.'

Some parameters are needed to enable managers to determine their priorities. May I suggest again the now-familiar concentric circles of priority as an aid, based on the 'need to know' principle:

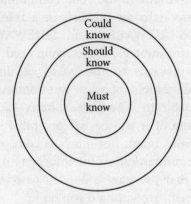

Priorities of 'need to know'

- MUST KNOW: vital points
- SHOULD KNOW: desirable but not essential
- COULD KNOW: relatively unimportant

MUST KNOW, for example, might include the introduction of a new product (downwards), the probability for good reason, for missing an important and agreed deadline (upwards), or the interest of a major customer in a service offered by a colleague's department (sideways). You might communicate these in a meeting or over the telephone, backed by the necessary paperwork. The fortunes of the organization's football team, as a COULD KNOW, should be left to the noticeboard or newsletter. SHOULD KNOW material should be mainly written or available on the computer screen. You should ensure that any form of face-to-face communication in meetings – expensive in terms of time and money – is reserved for essential, important or strategic messages and information in *each* of the three circles and NOT just the task.

I say that because all the pressures are on managers to reduce communication to short-term and bottom-line issues. That is one reason why the world now needs business leaders, not managers.

One of the forgotten arts of communication is public speaking in the sense of strategic or operational leaders standing up alone in front of their people and talking to them about task, team and individual agendas, followed by some two-way discussion. Sending messages by email isn't quite the same!

Encouraging two-way communication

At times I received advice from friends, urging me to give up or curtail visits to troops. They correctly stated that, so far as the mass of men was concerned, I could never speak, personally, to more than a tiny percentage. They argued, therefore, that I was merely wearing myself out, without accomplishing anything significant, so far as the whole Army was concerned. With this I did not agree. In the first place I felt that through constant talking to enlisted men I gained accurate impressions of their state of mind. I talked to them about anything and everything: a favourite question of mine was to inquire whether the particular squad or platoon had figured out any new trick or gadget for use in infantry fighting. I would talk about anything so long as I could get the soldier to talk to me in return.

I knew, of course, that news of a visit with even a few men in a division would soon spread throughout the unit. This, I felt, would encourage men to talk to their superiors, and this habit, I believe, promotes efficiency. There is, among the mass of individuals who carry the rifles in war, a great amount of ingenuity and initiative. If men can naturally and without restraint talk to their officers, the products of their resource-fulness becomes available to all. Moreover, out of the habit grows mutual confidence, a feeling of partnership that is the essence of esprit de corps. An army fearful of its officers is never as good as one that trusts and confides in its leaders.

General Dwight D. Eisenhower, former US President

It is sometimes difficult to get people together in this way, especially if you are not the chief executive. But you should seize every opportunity of talking – and listening – to any significant groups of those who report indirectly to you.

There are frequent attempts, some more successful than others, to systematic downward, upward and sideways communication by a series of regular meetings, such as briefing groups, liaison committees and works councils. Sometimes legislation directs managers to introduce a particular system, such as works councils.

There is always a temptation to believe that when you have introduced a *system* – such as briefing groups or works councils – you have solved the communication problem. But systems are subject to the law of atrophy: they tend to waste away. Systems can help, but they are as good as the people operating them. The winning combination is *simple but durable systems* peopled by *committed and skilled communi-cators*.it

Three possible aims for such consultative or representative meetings are:

- To give employees a chance to improve decisions by contributing comments before decisions are made.
- To make the fullest possible use of their experience and ideas in the efficient running of the enterprise.
- To give management and employees the opportunity to understand each other's views and objectives.

Characteristically these are meetings where discussion takes place on any matter influencing the effectiveness or efficiency of the enterprise prior to decisions being made. Sometimes the group's views will be passed upwards; sometimes the decision will be made by the manager on the spot and in the presence of those who have contributed to his or her judgement.

When managers do not listen they cease to be business leaders and revert to their former status as hired business administrators. So-called managers of this low calibre hardly listen at all: they *ignore, forget, distort* or *misunderstand* much of what they hear, as the case study below illustrates:

A large manufacturing company called Portland Power Units Ltd, makers of diesel engines, decide to invest in a large extension covering the adjacent car park. Mark Evans, the new manager in charge, drew up an elaborate plan for the change so as to minimize any disruption of production as the walls were knocked down. He rearranged the schedules and ordered the new machinery from a firm who had supplied them last time. The result was chaotic. The team leaders on the shop floor said they had not been consulted and the building works would certainly hold up an important new order for China. The union said that the shift schedules were unworkable. 'They could also have saved a lot of money and technical problems if they ordered the new German machinery we saw when we toured that plant in Frankfurt,' added one of the team leaders. Evans finally had to agree that he had not listened to those who knew most about the machinery, the layout of the new extension, the shift schedules or the timetable for building works. His poor listening cost Portland Power Units just under two million pounds. He is now working for another organization – possibly yours.

Remember that part of your skill as a communicator is to be aware of feedback – the part of your input that bounces back to you. It is useful because it helps you to judge whether or not communication is likely to be effective. Initial feedback – positive or negative – must be distinguished from the effect of the message as a whole (see 'The role of feedback', Chapter 1, page 15). 'It is interesting', one chief executive told me, 'that in business dealings we expect, and generally get, a response to every communication even though it be only an acknowledgement for a cheque; but in staff matters we are very often content to put a notice on the board and leave it at that.'

One of the advantages of getting out of your office (if you still have one) and going around talking to people is that you can gauge the flow of communication as it courses through the arteries and veins of the network:

- Did that message you asked operational leaders to brief to their team leaders reach *this* team in another country?
- Why didn't this key suggestion for a new extension of service to existing major customers get communicated to the senior leadership team?

- How come our Holland branch have cracked this particular production problem six months ago but when I was in Spain last week they were still struggling with it?
- Why hasn't this young graduate manager in Scotland heard about our new leadership development strategy?
- Don't these rumours and false reports suggest that we are falling down in communication? Is it a systems problem or a people problem?

Like the systems mentioned above, information technology – computers, email, television link-ups, mobile radios and video – will not solve your communication problems, they are only aids. Only by developing leaders at all three levels, and persuading them to work together as a team, will your organization be able to face the challenges of change and growth with confidence.

KEY POINTS: COMMUNICATING IN ORGANIZATIONS

- *To organize* implies arranging so that the whole aggregate works as a unit with each element having a proper function. In social bodies hierarchy and formal communication play a key role. *Organizations* are formal communication systems, open to their environment, with a definite purpose.
- The necessary content of communication within an organization is suggested by the Three Circles:
    TASK: The common purpose or vision, aims and objectives, strategy and plans, future prospects.
    TEAM: Issues to do with changes in organization or team work, how we can work better together.
    INDIVIDUAL: Anything that affects the individual for better or worse.

- Staying within the familiar spatial metaphor, there are *three main directions of flows of communication*: DOWN-WARDS, UPWARDS and SIDEWAYS. In times past, the emphasis fell on downwards communication from high to low. Now, for a variety of reasons, the formal communication system – supplemented by the informal one – has to bear information and ideas in *all three directions*. Therefore it has to become much more flexible in the future.

- As a general principle, high-priority information (the MUST as opposed to SHOULD or COULD know) should go by the best method of communication, which is *face-to-face backed by the written word*.

- As a leader you should not only place a high premium on good communication but become skilled in using the right method for it. Your role or appointment contains an inbuilt requirement to communicate in all three directions. In each direction you may be communicating self-generated ideas or acting as a transmitter – the latter is as important as the former.

- Systems, such as briefing groups or joint consultative councils, can all contribute, but remember that it is easier to set them up than to maintain them at a high level of effectiveness. Nor will information technology solve all your communication problems. Good communication requires good communicators. Which brings it back to YOU!

The major mistake in communication is to believe that it happens.

George Bernard Shaw, Irish playwright

CONCLUSION
EFFECTIVE COMMUNICATION

The major aim of this book has been to describe and explore the art of communication in such a way that you may feel inspired to set about a practical programme for improving your own communicating. Most of its pages have been devoted to the six elements that are present in any communication as depicted in the Communication Star: the *aim*, *communicator*, *communicant*, *content*, *methods* and *situation*. Awareness and understanding of these elements constitutes the first steps towards becoming better at communication.

The art of communication is essentially a practical one. It includes skills such as *speaking*, *listening*, *writing* and *reading*, which we all do but which few do excellently. These basic skills can all be improved by the conscious effort of applying the Five Principles of Good Speaking, also known as the Principles of Communication – Be Clear, Be Prepared, Be Simple, Be Vivid and Be Natural – to our daily practice of them.

Like learning a new language, this conscious phase may seem awkward and full of mistakes at first. But it is not unnatural, for art lies in perfecting our natural gifts. Eventually these efforts will drift into the subconscious mind and continue to influence attitudes and actions without us being fully conscious that they are doing so.

Through my writing of this book I have been aware that art, skill, craft and technique are only a part – although a vital part – of the answer. As in the cases of leadership and effective thinking, communication reserves its higher peaks of experience and achievement for those people who are touched already by what most of us must strive for with effort. Nor should we envy their ease and natural grace: they are the yardsticks and pacemakers for our own achievement. In them we see the restoration of that lost unity between the two meanings of the word *good*, namely, technical proficiency or skill in a craft on the one hand, and moral goodness and *integrity* on the other hand.

'The peoples of the world are islands shouting at each other across a sea of misunderstanding,' wrote the English author George Eliot, as quoted at the start of Chapter 1. It is this 'sea of misunderstanding' that isolates us as nations, organizations, groups and individuals into 'islands', defining our major problem for us.

Gradually, however, through the exercise of good leadership, served by our marvellous intellect and our unique potential for communication, those seas of chaos and misunderstanding may yet give way before us. And eventually we may build a new order on earth where it can be said, in the English poet John Donne's words: 'No man is an island, entire of itself, every man is a piece of the continent, a part of the main.'

INDEX

Page references in **Bold** denote complete chapters